An OPU

After Yeats

Neil Corcoran is Professor of English at the University of St Andrews. His books include *Seamus Heaney* (1986), *The Chosen Ground: Essays on the Contemporary Poetry of Northern Ireland* (1992), and *English Poetry Since 1940* (1993).

OPUS General Editors

Christopher Butler
Robert Evans
John Skorupski

OPUS books provide concise, original, and authoritative introductions to a wide range of subjects in the humanities and social sciences. They are written by experts for the general reader as well as for students.

After Yeats and Joyce

Reading Modern Irish Literature

Neil Corcoran

Oxford   New York

OXFORD UNIVERSITY PRESS

1997

Oxford University Press, Great Clarendon Street, Oxford OX2 6DP

Oxford New York
Athens Auckland Bangkok Bogota Bombay
Buenos Aires Calcutta Cape Town Dar es Salaam
Delhi Florence Hong Kong Istanbul Karachi
Kuala Lumpur Madras Madrid Melbourne
Mexico City Nairobi Paris Singapore
Taipei Tokyo Toronto

and associated companies in
Berlin Ibadan

Oxford is a trade mark of Oxford University Press

First published as an Oxford University Press paperback 1997

British Library Cataloguing in Publication Data
Data available

Library of Congress Cataloging in Publication Data
Corcoran, Neil.
After Yeats and Joyce: reading modern Irish literature/Neil
Corcoran.
"OPUS"—Ser. t.p.
Includes bibliographical references and index.
1. English literature—Irish authors—History and criticism.
2. Ireland—Intellectual life—20th century. 3. Yeats, W. B.
(William Butler), 1865–1939—Influence. 4. Joyce, James, 1882–1941—
Influence. 5. Ireland—In literature. I. Title.
PR8753.C665 1997 (820.9'9415'0904—dc21) (97-2971)
ISBN 0-19-289231-2

1 3 5 7 9 10 8 6 4 2

Typeset by Best-set Typesetter Ltd., Hong Kong
Printed in Great Britain by
Biddles Ltd
Guildford and King's Lynn

Preface

This is a book about Irish literature after Yeats and Joyce and it is, therefore, a book about texts which have been the subject of much critical contention. The contention begins with the phrase 'Irish literature' itself which, to some, should still be reserved for works in the Irish language. These continue to be written in modern Ireland, and they inherit a very rich history with particular high points in the Middle Ages and the eighteenth century. For a long time the phrase 'Anglo-Irish literature' was used—and still is by some critics, literary historians, and literary syllabuses—as a way of distinguishing from, and perhaps also tactfully deferring to literature in the Irish language. However, this term has political and ethnographical connotations which, in my opinion, make it inappropriate to a great deal of the literature which I actually discuss in this book. Some critics have tried different ways of overcoming or ducking the terminological difficulty. The use of the term 'Irish writing' is common, and this is usually also intended to suggest the way in which the category of literature is interwoven with other categories of writing, including the political and the critical-theoretical; but the frequency of its use has by now made it seem a little jaded. Seamus Deane, in his *Short History of Irish Literature*, however, takes what Bruce Stewart has described as a 'benchmark' taxonomic initiative, employing the term 'Irish literature' to refer now to Irish literature in English. I follow suit in that, taking heart from Stewart's unillusioned acerbity: 'There is a time to call a halt to all of that.'[1]

I do so, however, in full knowledge of what has sometimes been involved here, which Stewart categorizes as 'a world of often fierce antagonisms invoking the pride and anxieties of a tragically suppressed (yet partially resuscitated) native language, and the hauteur and unease of a forcibly imposed yet fully assimilated one, each wearing the uncompromising aspect of a manichean hero as they face up to each other in fatal dispute over the body of Ireland'.[2] The fact, that is to say, that the Irish language was almost eradicated during the nineteenth century is still, however few people actually now speak or write it in contemporary Ireland, an inescapable fact of Irish history and Irish literary history. Since its eradication was, at least in part, a matter of political coercion or duress—the 'national school' system prohibited the speaking of Irish—and also, in part, a matter of the tragic history of the vast scale of emigration which followed on the Irish Famine of 1845–8, the disappearance of the language persists, even among many of those who do not possess it, as a painful absence associated with the major catastrophes of colonial history. In this sense, as Thomas Kinsella has memorably phrased it, 'it is one of the findings of Ireland's dual tradition that an empire is a passing thing, but that a colony is not'.[3] This is why, among Irish writers who write in the English language, language itself—the material actually used—characteristically becomes the focus of scrutiny and reflection, sometimes in a heavily emphatic or foregrounded way. It is also why translation from Irish into English, and various other kinds of translation too, together with ideas or theories of the process of translation itself, have such significance in the literature of this period. Hence my decision to open this book with an account of the issue, in the chapter entitled 'Translations', where I have more to say about the fate of the Irish language.

In that chapter, and in those that follow, it is also part of my aim to describe some of the ways in which literature in English in Ireland has been, in the period since Yeats and Joyce, a literature in which ideas of Ireland—of people, community and nation—have been both created and reflected, and in which conceptions of a distinctively Irish identity have been articulated, defended, and challenged. Irish literature in this period is characteristically a literature of process and becoming, the ground of debate, contestation, and renewal, the scene of an intertextuality in which Ireland is itself read. I have therefore entitled this book *After Yeats and Joyce* for two reasons. The first is simply chronological: the literature discussed here is that of those writers who follow on the achievements of the two major figures who stand at the entrance to the Irish twentieth century. Chronologically this book therefore begins in the early 1920s, when Yeats's reputation was well consolidated and when Joyce published *Ulysses* (in 1922). This was also the period of the immediate aftermath of the revolutionary energy initiated by the Easter Rising of 1916. After the War of Independence of 1919–21,[4] a treaty between Britain and Ireland was signed which ratified the terms of the Government of Ireland Act of 1920, providing for the establishment of the Irish Free State as a Dominion of the British Commonwealth (it became the Republic in 1949 and withdrew from the Commonwealth) and which led to the establishment of a separate devolved parliament for the six north-eastern counties of Ireland (Antrim, Armagh, Derry, Down, Fermanagh, and Tyrone). That treaty provoked, in 1922–3, a bloody civil war between its supporters and opponents. The literature I discuss here has its origins, then, in a time of intense political turmoil, and it often returns to these origins. However, it customarily evokes too a period of post-revolutionary disillusionment or stasis in the Free State and Republic itself, and it sometimes articulates or reflects the sense of historical inconclusiveness which followed in the wake of Partition in 1921.

This literature is also 'after Yeats and Joyce', however, in the aesthetic or intertextual sense: it is, that is to say, a literature always to some degree shadowed by the achievements of these un-ignorable turn-of-the-century writers, a literature having to come to terms with belatedness or subsequence. This is, as the following chapters frequently make clear, sometimes a matter of direct allusion. It is also sometimes a matter of stylistic or thematic indebtedness, and this is not necessarily genre-specific. Yeats, for instance, primarily a poet, is a central presence in the tradition of the 'Big House' novel which I define in Chapter 2, and Joyce, primarily a novelist, has been so deeply influential on a range of modern and contemporary poets as to make the title of one critical study, *Irish Poetry after Joyce*, not self-evidently an absurdity.[5] Tracing this kind of intertextuality is to discover how subsequence may be turned to inventive and fertile advantage, how a great virtue may be made of an alarming necessity. In the texts discussed in this book the work and personalities of Yeats and Joyce run a gamut of response: imitation, admiration, dependency, modification, hesitation, anxiety, separation, subversion, rejection, reaction. It is a rich intertextual tale.

This literature is shadowed not only by the work of Yeats and Joyce, however, but also by what has frequently been read as the antagonism between them, where the election of one has often involved the depreciation of the other. This does seem to me a genuine affect in creative writing of the period, but it is also, more obviously, a strain in modern Irish criticism. Yeats steps forward into modernity out of the mists of the Celtic twilight and the Irish Literary Revival, and is therefore always suspect to some as the purveyor of erroneous and dangerous Anglo-Irish myths about Ireland, the West, the peasantry, and the 'traditional'. Joyce, on the other hand, is read as urban realist, European modernist, stylistic revolutionary. Other oppositions also form part of the adversarial plot: Yeats is élitist or fascist, Joyce is democratic or socialist; Yeats is a magical mythologist, static, hieratic, and tragic, Joyce is—for all his Ovidian and Homeric paralleling—provisional, deconstructive, ironic, and comic. Terence Brown has summarized this critical tradition in an essay in which he finds it present as a mode of perception, or of prejudice, in Irish critical writing from Daniel Corkery's seminal books *The Hidden Ireland* (1924) and *Synge and Anglo-Irish Literature* (1931)—where the role of Joyce, who had not impacted on Corkery, is played by Synge—through the influential criticism of Thomas Kinsella in the later 1960s, up to Seamus Deane and other members of the Field Day enterprise in recent times.[6] It may well be, nevertheless, that this is virtually the terminal point at which this literature need feel so obliged. Seamus Heaney—who has, it could be said, translated this adversarial debate into some of the very terms of reference of his own poetry and criticism—has recently written of the 'unconsoled modernity' of Yeats's achievement, reading it as 'an energy released and a destiny discharged';[7] and W. J.

McCormack has pointed one way out of the by-now routinely reflex impasse by diagnosing both Yeats and Joyce as the dual inheritors of 'a history of embarrassment', of various forms of Irish shame or depredation which they turn into artistic pride—in Yeats 'the pride of heroic overcoming', in Joyce that of 'devious transfiguration'.[8] Such alignments of the two may eventually produce newly complicated and possibly newly enabling critical readings and creative responses.

If reactions to Yeats and Joyce provide an overarching theme for this book, I have organized my study of this literature into specific thematic chapters too. I do not claim any great originality for the themes I discuss here; indeed, to do so would make a nonsense of my design, which is to describe themes actually persistent in Irish literature in the period, to which individual writers recur frequently, and often with a strong awareness of one another's work. One of my aims in the book, then, is to indicate something of the intense degree of cross-fertilization there is in this literature. The thematic approach also makes it possible to suggest the range of interest of some of the most significant writers, whose texts feature in different chapters and, I would argue, accrete critical resonance and complexity from these varied juxtapositions and alignments. This may be thought particularly true of the work of Northern Irish writers, which figures both in a separate chapter and elsewhere too. I hope this is not a side-stepping of the question of where this work really fits under the rubric of 'Irish literature', but in fact a view of where it fits: it has a history unique to itself, and requires its own context to make that plain; but it is also part of another history in ways that become clear once the collocations are made. I am aware, of course, that the Irish literary histories that will be written in future may well turn on how and where this work is placed. The post-colonial model for Irish writing proposed in such books as David Lloyd's *Anomalous States* is, while admitted to have certain relevances, contested by some critics whose sense of the impact of Northern writing, and its complication of the Irish/English relation, is most acute.[9] This may be the sharpest point, but it is nevertheless only one of the many points at which, in relation to modern Irish literature, the literary is a category always osmotic to politics and cultural politics. My themes are chosen with this very much in mind: a theme, the literary historian David Perkins has said, is 'especially the point at which literature interacts with extra-literary conditions'.[10] This is my point too: which is why I hope to have historicized these themes as thoroughly as I can while still discussing individual texts as literary entities and organisms.

I am very grateful to Christopher Butler, Patrick Crotty, Rik Kavanagh, Bernard O'Donoghue, and two anonymous OUP readers for offering advice on earlier drafts of this book. Without their perceptive comments and beady eyes it would be leaving my hands with even less confidence than it does. I am also most grateful to the Principal and Fellows of St John's College, Oxford, for their award of a Visiting Scholarship which enabled a period of sustained work in the Bodleian Library at a very useful time. I acknowledge too the Society of Authors for a generous grant towards research costs which made possible a period of work in Ireland. The Research Funds of the University of Sheffield and the University of Wales, Swansea, were also supportive.

Neil Corcoran

In memory of my father,
John Patrick Corcoran

. . . taking your own pulse
And counting in you someone else.

Contents

1

Translations

1. Acquired Speech

In the final section of James Joyce's *A Portrait of the Artist as a Young Man* (1916) Stephen Dedalus walks the streets of Dublin quoting Ben Jonson, considering the 'heaps of dead language' on advertising hoardings, and meditating on the haunting story of sexual invitation and refusal recently told him by his friend Davin, the rural student nationalist and speaker of Irish, for whom Stephen has a tenderness quite exceptional in his relationships with his peers. After emblematizing the pregnant woman of Davin's story as 'a type of her race and his own, a batlike soul waking to the consciousness of itself in darkness and secrecy and loneliness', Stephen has an interview in his university college with the Jesuit dean of studies who is, like many of those who taught in the Royal University of Ireland in its early years, an Englishman. During their conversation Stephen uses the word 'tundish' where the dean would use 'funnel':

—Is that called a tundish in Ireland? asked the dean. I never heard the word in my life.
—It is called a tundish in Lower Drumcondra, said Stephen laughing, where they speak the best English.
—A tundish, said the dean reflectively. That is a most interesting word. I must look that word up. Upon my word I must.

The exchange prompts in Stephen a meditation on the difference between the language he speaks and that spoken by the Englishman which has become a classic text in modern Irish critical writing—cited perhaps almost too frequently—for the humiliations endured by a colonized people when they must speak the language of the colonial oppressor:

The little word seemed to have turned a rapier point of his sensitiveness against this courteous and vigilant foe. He felt with a smart of dejection that the man to whom he was speaking was a countryman of Ben Jonson. He thought:

—The language in which we are speaking is his before it is mine. How different are the words *home*, *Christ*, *ale*, *master*, on his lips and on mine! I cannot speak or write these words without unrest of spirit. His language, so familiar and so foreign, will always be for me an acquired speech. I have not made or accepted its words. My voice holds them at bay. My soul frets in the shadow of his language.

At the very end of the book, as Stephen prepares to leave Ireland for voluntary exile in France, he records in his diary his own consultation of the English dictionary—with, presumably, a sly dig at the dean's conventional but culpable falsity of manner here, which may register a snobbish condescension towards the Irishman's idiom: his mild oath ('Upon my word') insists too much for us to assume that he has any real intention of looking the word up. The diary entry, for 13 April, records the relentlessness of Stephen's intellectual pursuit of a means of overcoming his original shame:

That tundish has been on my mind for a long time. I looked it up and find it English and good old blunt English too. Damn the dean of studies and his funnel! What did he come here for to teach us his own language or to learn it from us? Damn him one way or the other![1]

At first humiliated by the language he speaks, Stephen turns his humiliation into venomous attack, and his weapon is the English dictionary. Looking up 'tundish' there, Joyce himself would have discovered that it is truly what Stephen embarrassedly and self-mockingly calls 'the best English', or at least the more venerable English, since it, rather than 'funnel', is the language of the Elizabethans and has significant literary sanction. 'Tundish' figures in Shakespeare's *Measure for Measure*, and is first recorded in the fourteenth century, whereas 'funnel' is a fifteenth-century French derivation. The dictionary therefore provides a lesson in Irish colonial history, since the word 'tundish' was clearly transported to Ireland during the Elizabethan Plantation of the country, or earlier; but it also turns the

humiliation of that history into linguistic triumph, sanctioning a
new pride in the language Stephen, and Joyce, actually speak,
the language now known by linguists as 'Hiberno-English'.
Ulysses, the book Joyce writes in his Parisian 'silence, exile and
cunning', subsequently becomes a virtual encyclopedia of this
language. Making English, in the terms of the *Portrait*, at once
both familiar and foreign, the novel comes into almost explicit
competition with Shakespeare in its lexical variety and figurative
inventiveness. Given the arrogance required for the effort, it
would not have surprised Joyce to learn that the current Oxford
English Dictionary cites *A Portrait of the Artist as a Young Man*
along with *Measure for Measure* as one of its sources for the
word 'tundish': the whirligig of time bringing in its revenges.

It may be thought that in his final book *Finnegans Wake*
(1939) Joyce pursues such subversive revenge on the English
language even further, making it astonishingly and uniquely
foreign to itself by more or less retaining its syntax while radically destabilizing its lexicon in a promiscuous riot of pun and
word-play. In the 'language in no sinse of the world' of the *Wake*
English is exposed to numerous other languages in a way that
undermines the assertiveness of its imperial authority, or
de-authorizes it. Etymology in the *Wake*, as Seamus Deane has
suggested, becomes the agency of an antagonistic politics, one
that refuses the containment of English identity and does so
from a position of radical estrangement.[2] In cosmopolitan European exile Joyce is enabled to write an English which some
commentators regard as the ultimate manifestation of his complex feelings about being an Irish writer who does not write in
the Irish language. In the *Portrait* Stephen's objection to the
dean's English is that 'I did not make its words'; in the *Wake*
Joyce makes his own instead: 'Are we speachin d'anglas
landadge or are you sprakin sea Djoytsch?'

Joyce's politics are antagonistic not only to the power of the
English, however, but also to the proffered alternatives of the
Irish nationalism of his day. If the exuberantly varied Hiberno-
English of *Ulysses* everywhere expresses Joyce's refusal of any
'standard' English, it also offers scathing satires of perceived and

advertised ideas of Irishness. The 'Cyclops' episode of the novel, with its elaborate parodies of various Irish nationalist rhetorics, is a hyperbolically sustained rebuke to the hypocrisies and fanaticisms of a monocular, anti-Semitic Irish nationalism which has at its source a sentimental, perverse, and opportunistic commitment to a 'return' to the language. Similarly, in the book's opening episode, 'Telemachus', Joyce even-handedly also satirizes what he regards as the pretensions and affectations of those versions of Irish folklore and mythology which characterized the effort towards a national literature in the work of the Irish Literary Revival of the turn of the century, notably in Yeats's book *The Celtic Twilight* (1893).

In this episode Haines, an Oxford student friend of Buck Mulligan's, is in Ireland in order to learn Irish as a result of his interest in the writings of the Revival, but his self-satisfied ignorance and fatuity earn only contempt from Stephen. In various ways 'Telemachus' promotes Joyce's view that the revival of Irish is little more than part of the contemporary European taste for the folkloric, having scant regard for actual Irish economic and linguistic realities. The old milkwoman in the episode, who speaks so little Irish that she thinks Haines's few words of it are French, is transformed in Stephen's imagination into a latter-day version of the *cailleach*, or hag figure, of early Irish poetry, a representative of Ireland itself, now pathetically but also venally humbled, 'the lowly form of an immortal, serving her conqueror and her gay betrayer'. The Englishman Haines is her conqueror; the Irishman Mulligan, who cheerfully peddles for financial and social gain a Revivalist version of Irishness conveniently sanitized for English consumption, is her betrayer. The Stephen of *Ulysses* will neither serve nor betray, even if that has the inevitable consequence of lifelong exile.

Recent commentators have argued for the genuine scholarship of Yeats's recoveries of Gaelic material, despite his lack of any knowledge of the Irish language, and for their political antagonism to certain stereotypical ideas of the 'Celt' (notably Matthew Arnold's).[3] But to Joyce the entire effort seemed all too easily assimilable to such stereotypes, rendering the Celt (or

the Irishman) powerless by rendering him fey, folksy, and whim-
sically superstitious. In *Finnegans Wake* the decorous, *fin-de-
siècle* politeness of the phrase 'Celtic twilight' is travestied by the
insinuatingly obscene word-play which renders it as the 'cultic
twalette'. The translations and versions of the Revival, however,
remain persistently present to subsequent Irish writers in English who would draw material from the cultural deposits of the
Irish language, but so also does the Joycean antagonism. If it has
been possible for some Irish writers to rest more or less content
with George Bernard Shaw's brusque pragmatism—'English is
the native language of Irishmen'[4]—numerous others have been
shadowed by the dilemma Yeats announces, with its intimations
of confusion and loss, when he says that 'Gaelic is my national
language, but it is not my mother tongue'.[5]

2. *Linguistic Contours*

One of the best-known and most controversial examinations of
the 'language issue' in modern Irish writing is Brian Friel's play
Translations, first performed in 1980, which dramatizes the dilemma at its point of origin, but also from the perspective of its
present moment. A historical drama set in the fictional community of Ballybeg in Co. Donegal in 1833, the play examines the
effects on the community of the Ordnance Survey made at the
time which mapped and surveyed Ireland and translated Irish
place-names into English, and of the contemporaneous introduction of a system of 'national schools', which were to educate
hitherto Irish-speaking children entirely through English. The
play attempts to stage, then, the tensions of the moment at which
the old Irish civilization is 'translated' into the dominant British
colonial culture. It is set in a 'hedge-school', where the classics of
Greek and Latin literature are taught by the drunken and pomp-
ous Hugh O'Donnell, helped by his lame son Manus: such
schools, held in rural barns or sheds, were a heritage of the Penal
Laws in Ireland (*c*.1690–1795) which forbade an official education to Catholic children. Hugh's other son, Owen, has spent six
years in Dublin and is now working as an interpreter for the

Royal Engineers, a regiment of the British Army, in their task of surveying. His immediate dealings are with the stiff imperialist Captain Lancey and the sympathetic Lieutenant Yolland, who is becoming a devotee of the topography, community, and language of Ballybeg.

The play's plot centres on the developing relationship between Yolland and Maire, a student at the school involved in an apparently failing liaison with Manus. The relationship culminates in Yolland's presumed abduction and murder by the always absent, but much mentioned, Donnelly twins, who are, it seems, resolutely anti-English and subversive of all the Engineers' efforts. After Yolland's disappearance, the previously uneasy tolerance between the army and the Ballybeg locals collapses under the threat of Draconian army reprisals. The play ends indeterminately with the army camp set on fire and with Owen, realizing the ignominy of his role as go-between, leaving with the apparent intention of joining the Donnellys. Hugh has the closing speech, in which he remembers his lack of heroism during the rebellion against English rule in Ireland in 1798. Offering to teach English to the distraught Maire, he ends quoting Virgil on the fall of Troy to the Greeks, offering an implicit analogy with the British imperial power in Ireland.

As that ending makes plain, this plot is the vehicle for an elaboration of the various kinds of 'translation' suggested by the play's title. Prominent among these is the dramatic irony that the Irish characters, although they speak English on stage, must be presumed to be speaking Irish. This is the most obvious instance of the way the linguistic culture represented by Ballybeg has in fact terminated: the Ireland in which the play was first produced is, of course, an almost entirely Anglophone country (although the city in which it was first performed still has two names, depending on your affiliations and allegiances: 'Derry', which translates the Irish 'Doire', meaning 'oak wood', or 'Londonderry', which dominates the Irish with the name of the English capital city: hence the popular way of referring to the place— 'London/Derry'—as 'Stroke City'). This linguistic irony reaches a poignant intensity in the play's central scene, in which Maire and Yolland, without sharing a language, still manage to communicate their love for each other by displaying a reverent tenderness for the place-names of their different native areas—her Ballybeg, his Norfolk—as they repeat them in an affectionate litany. The irony is that their deep understanding is not dependent on language—'Don't stop—I know what you're saying', says Maire—where elsewhere the attempt at translation leads only to violence. Owen's opportunistic collaboration in the Survey is radically opposed, prior to Yolland's disappearance, by Manus, who considers it 'a bloody military operation': which is of course what it soon literally becomes. The play's conclusion sets Owen's self-disgust over against Hugh's earlier apparent realism. Having articulated a theory of the Irish language as the luxurious response to material deprivation ('full of the mythologies of fantasy and hope and self-deception—a syntax opulent with tomorrows'), he says that 'words are signals, counters. They are not immortal. And it can happen . . . that a civilisation can be imprisoned in a linguistic contour which no longer matches the landscape of . . . fact.'[6]

Serious objection has been made, notably by the historian Sean Connolly, to the way Friel uses historical evidence in *Translations*, concerning both the Survey and the introduction of the national school system, and this case has not been satisfactorily countered.[7] Even so, Friel is manifestly himself also translating this past into his own contemporary present, since some crucial speeches in the play, including Hugh's final one, are taken more or less verbatim from George Steiner's study of the nature of translation, *After Babel* (1975). If its strong element of contemporary reference has led some critics to read *Translations* as a covert allegory of the British Army's presence in Northern Ireland (with the Donnelly twins representing the IRA), it also proposes that the matter of linguistic change from Irish to English, and the ways in which the old culture may be considered to survive a change of language, are still very living issues in Ireland. 'Confusion is not an ignoble condition', Hugh says; but the play may well itself be confused in its failure to judge between Hugh's realism about the fate of Irish and the emotional investment it seems to make in Yolland's outsider sense that the old culture contained 'a consciousness that wasn't striving or agitated, but at its ease and with its own conviction and assurance'. Similarly, *Translations* has little to say to those who would maintain that the language was in any case bound to die, victim of the internal pressures of necessary emigration to English-speaking countries and the desire for social status. Nevertheless, the dramatic force of the play's key moments offers a vivid interrogation in modern Irish writing of some of the ways in which people are, as Hugh says (again quoting Steiner), shaped by 'images of the past embodied in language': an aim fully in harmony with the cultural programme of the Field Day Theatre Company which *Translations* initiated.

This inspection of images also suggests that Friel's play derives from an awareness of the fate of the Irish language at the hands of succeeding Irish governments after 1923, which insisted that it should once again become, officially, the first language of the state. Generations of schoolchildren in the Republic were required to pass examinations in it in order to proceed to higher education and a range of jobs; and it was also on the syllabuses of Roman Catholic schools in Northern Ireland. Until the 1970s, when the examination requirements were effectively ended, this proved, unsurprisingly, a deterrent to general interest and, consequently, to significant literary achievement; and it also made Irish seem often the language only of the conformist or the opportunist. Some notable work was, nevertheless, produced in the language in the intervening period, such as the poetry of Seán O Riordáin, Máirtín O Direáin, and Máire Mhac an tSaoi and the novel *Cré na Cille* [*Churchyard Clay*] (1949) by Máirtín O Cadhain, which offers a telling trope for the state of the 'national' language at the time: its characters are talking corpses in a graveyard in Connemara.[8] In general, however, the facts of state coercion and conservative affiliation made it an unlikely literary vehicle for contemporary Irish experience.

In the 1970s, however, with the dropping of the old requirements, a sophisticated and politically liberal or radical generation turned again to the language. Associated with the journal

Innti in Cork, such poets as Michael Davitt and Nuala Ní Dhomnaill have since brought unpredictably secular and cosmopolitan energies, tones, and preoccupations into writing in the Irish language, replacing nationalist attachments with counter-cultural subversiveness. These have been acknowledged by a contemporary generation of Irish poets writing in English, to the extent that Davitt's poem 'An Scathán', translated as 'The Mirror', is one of the high points of Paul Muldoon's volume *Quoof* (1983), and Ní Dhomnaill has been translated by a constellation of poets in *Pharaoh's Daughter* (1990) and extensively by Muldoon alone in *The Astrakhan Cloak* (1992). These translations in effect make Ní Dhomnaill as significant in English as she is in Irish and represent one of the most fruitful recent *rapprochements* between the two literatures: most appropriately so for a writer who herself, in such poems as 'Feeding a Child' and 'The Unfaithful Wife', produces a hybrid in which myth, legend, and folklore come into edgy correspondence with a sceptical, satirical, erotic, and feminist sensibility and a contemporary urban consciousness. The poems, dealing with such subjects as adultery, anorexia, and a dissatisfaction with orthodox Catholicism, have a bravely and brashly cavalier disregard for the inherited Irish pieties. Their fairy women wield Black-and-Decker drills; the Shan Van Vocht, that ancient symbol of nationalist disaffection, appears as a 'cranky, cantankerous' old woman; the Great Queen Medb from the Ulster heroic mythological cycle berates the hero Cuchulain as a 'ball-less little bollocks' afraid of her *vagina dentata*. The poem translated by Muldoon as 'The Language Issue' explicitly proposes a hope for Irish which is elsewhere always implicit in the 'issue', or production, of her own, now in effect bilingual, poems:

> I place my hope on the water
> in this little boat
> of the language . . .
>
> only to have it borne hither and thither,
> not knowing where it might end up;
> in the lap, perhaps,
> of some Pharaoh's daughter.[9]

Tentativeness here meets an almost arrogant optimism: since in the Book of Exodus it is of course Moses who falls into the lap of Pharaoh's daughter, saved so that he may eventually lead his people into the Promised Land.

However, the kind of renewal of the language proposed by this conceit encounters many antagonistic attitudes too in modern Irish writing. Paula Meehan, in the poem 'Ard Fheis', for instance, from her volume *The Man who was Marked by Winter* (1991), is taken to a 'ghost place' by the sound of the language, 'a cobwebby state, chilled vault I littered with our totems', the now calcified emblems of a repressive Catholic Republic; and Eavan Boland, in 'Mise Eire' in her book *The Journey* (1987)— the title means 'I am Ireland' and alludes to the famous poem by Padraig Pearse and to the music by Seán O Riada written to commemorate the Easter Rising of 1916—insists that she 'won't go back to it— I my nation displaced I into old dactyls', preferring instead to put her faith in such images of resourceful womanhood as that of a nineteenth-century emigrant with her child on board ship for America, confident that 'a new language I is a kind of scar I and heals after a while I into a passable imitation I of what went before'. Between such kinds of commitment and rejection, however, there is the third way offered in a great deal of modern Irish writing by the complex and always to some degree controversial idea of 'translation'.

3. *English Irishes*

Many Irish writers who use English embody in different ways in their work a consciousness of linguistic otherness. This may take the relatively reticent form of a subtle or sly employment of Hiberno-English idiom. Seamus Heaney discovers such an instance in Patrick Kavanagh's poem 'Inniskeen Road, July Evening', where 'the bicycles go by in twos and threes', rather than 'pass by' or 'go past', as they would in more standard English. Kavanagh, Heaney says, 'is letting the very life blood of the place in that one minute incision'.[10] His own work contains such incisions too, as in 'The Strand at Lough Beg', where the

Hiberno-English form of the past habitual tense ('used' rather than 'used to') acts as a linguistic rapport between Heaney the poet and his elegized farm-labourer cousin, the murdered Colum McCartney ('There you used hear guns fired behind the house | Long before rising time').[11] Elsewhere in his work, in such poems as 'The Backward Look', 'Alphabets', and 'A Shooting Script', Heaney both celebrates and elegizes the Irish language, and he also makes some of its persistences within the English spoken in his native County Derry part of the figurative apparatus of the books *Wintering Out* (1972) and *North* (1975), notably in what have become known as his 'place-name poems'. Such pieces as 'Anahorish', 'Toome', and 'Broagh' establish continuity with the Irish form known as *dinnseanchas*, poems which explore the etymologies and associations of place-names. *Wintering Out* employs a range of Heaney's own Co. Derry dialect words as emblems of a shared communal consciousness in the early days of conflict in Northern Ireland; and he uses specifically Hiberno-English forms such as the phrase 'bite 'n' sup', handled with striking tenderness and pathos in the volume's dedicatory poem. Paul Muldoon's English is similarly ghosted by some kinds of Irish usage, notably the employment of the present habitual tense 'would', a common tense in the Irish language. This is one way in which his work characteristically effects what Edna Longley has called its 'distrust of the definitive'.[12]

In a more foregrounded, and rather more self-conscious way, Tom Paulin, who discusses some of these issues in his essay 'A New Look at the Language Question' in his collection *Ireland and the English Crisis* (1984), uses a range of what he tells us are the dialect words of Northern Irish Planter English, particularly in its Ulster Scots forms (words such as 'senna', 'biffy', 'glooby', 'screggy', and so on), and Frances Molloy, in her novel *No Mate for the Magpie* (1985), experimentally disrupts English orthography in order to write a novel in the Ulster patois of its subjective narrator. Such uses of dialect and disruption manifestly serve either a cultural idea or a class affiliation; and this is true too of the orthographical variations in the plays of such writers as Sean

O'Casey and Brendan Behan, and in narrative fictions representing a primarily uneducated or working class, such as the
'Barrytown' trilogy of Roddy Doyle. These transcriptions of
Irish speech possess great verve and immediacy, but there is
sometimes the danger that they will seem 'stage-Irish', not because they appear ridiculous to foreign ears, but, more insidi-
ously, because their charm invites a certain condescension. Jack
Boyle's famous observation that 'the whole counthry's in a state
o' chassis' in O'Casey's *Juno and the Paycock* (1925) is perhaps
a case in point.

Beyond such absorptions and assimilations, however, there
has also, particularly since the Revival, been a persistent desire
among Irish writers to carry over into English something of the
Irish texts themselves.[13] A number of the issues involved in this
were influentially explored in 'The Divided Mind', an essay by
Thomas Kinsella, in 1973. The Irish writer, he thought then,
could never be properly 'at home' in the English tradition, cut
off as he or she was by the silence of the nineteenth century from
the riches of the Irish-language tradition which had died in the
eighteenth. The result was a perceived sense of loss and discon-
tinuity, the 'divided mind' of a dual heritage and allegiance. The
paradoxical sustenance in this for the Irish writer was, nevertheless, that it could be read as one among several such models for
all writers in the modern world, who are notably 'the inheritors
of a gapped, discontinuous, polyglot tradition'.[14] Kinsella, that is
to say, is fully aware in the essay of what has sometimes been
offered as a criticism of it: that he is describing an actuality in
modern experience, if with a particular Irish inflection, at least
as much as he is proposing a cultural fact about the past.

When he introduces his *New Oxford Book of Irish Verse* in
1986, however, his tone is markedly more optimistic than it is in
'The Divided Mind'. 'The Irish tradition', he now claims, 'is a
matter of two linguistic entities in dynamic interaction, of two
major bodies of poetry asking to be understood together as
functions of a shared and painful history.'[15] Kinsella is implicitly
justifying his own practice here, since his work has been at the
centre of recent retrievals or repossessions of Irish-language

literary culture. His translations of Irish verse from the earliest times to the eighteenth century form a large part of his *Oxford Book*; he is the translator of *The Táin* (1969), the ancient, appallingly violent Irish epic of Medb and Cuchulain, from the Ulster cycle of mythical material also much drawn upon by Yeats; and he is editor and translator (with Sean O Tuama) of the anthology *An Duanaire: 1600–1800: Poems of the Dispossessed* (1981), which gave new impetus to the reading and study of Irish-language poetry from the elegiac period before its demise, and brought to a new readership a range of well-known *aisling* poems by such writers as Aodhagán O Rathaille, in which Ireland is encountered in an allegorical vision as a beautiful woman, and in which political hope is invested in a Jacobite redeemer. There are many instances in modern Irish writing where the *aisling* form is adapted, accommodated, or parodied (such as those poems actually entitled 'Aisling' by Austin Clarke, Seamus Heaney, and Paul Muldoon).

Kinsella's creative work as a poet draws heavily on his efforts and ambitions as a translator. His poems frequently figure dream-like or nightmare states in which Irish historical experience and mythological motifs are interwoven with images from the creative and psychological life. In 'The Route of the Táin', for instance, in his volume *Notes from the Land of the Dead* (1973), he attempts to follow the journey taken by the armies of the epic as they prepare for battle. Echoes of his translation of *The Táin* occur, but now in a context of allegorical self-reference, as the poet-translator discovers in this reworking of the original material something 'shivering suddenly into meaning | along new boundaries'. Similarly, his work sometimes draws out personal and political implications from the images of the *cailleach* and of the scribe prominent in Irish heroic and medieval poetry. His translation in the *Oxford Book* of the early Irish poem 'The Hag of Beare', for instance, feeds into the imagery of the poem 'Hen Woman' in *Notes from the Land of the Dead*, which concerns his own grandmother. Read in tandem, the two poems suggest a continuity in masculine Irish forms of feeling about maternal figures. Similarly, the numerous

monastic poems of the *Oxford Book* inform his self-image as
poet in 'St. Catherine's Clock' in *Blood and Family* (1988),
performing 'a scribal act on the skin' of a vellum manuscript
which may be, masochistically, the writer's own skin too.

These 'new boundaries' of feeling and meaning, in which
elements of the Irish-language tradition are repossessed by a
penetratingly modern sensibility and consciousness, are also
sought out in Kinsella's lengthy, continuing sequence of
'Peppercanister poems', of which 'St. Catherine's Clock' forms
part. Deriving some structural possibilities from Ezra Pound's
Cantos, the sequence is a fragmented inquiry into heritage, origin, and source in ways which experimentally cross personal
biography or psychodrama with an attempt at a definition of
national identity. The individual poems in the sequence seek out
what one of them, 'Songs of the Psyche', calls 'the subsequent |
bustling in the previous'. The paralleling of interior and exterior
worlds is at its most acute in 'Finistere', which links an account
of psychological and creative anxiety or accidie with the imagery
of the very early Irish text known as *The Book of Invasions*.
Writing partly in the persona of the legendary first Irish poet
Amergin, Kinsella creates here a poem whose English takes into
itself the most ancient extant Irish literary material, effecting
thereby not only a contemporary repossession of the past but
also a demonstration of the way the poet is himself possessed by
that past. His work dramatizes the labour of 'searching in its own
tissue | for the structure | in which it may wake'.

Kinsella's is possibly the most prominent and rigorous attempt at the act of repossession in modern Irish writing, and one
of the most highly regarded, but it is by no means unique. The
short-story writer Frank O'Connor was deeply influential on
Kinsella's own generation with his translations of such poems
as Brian Merriman's eighteenth-century *The Midnight Court*
(1945), his *Kings, Lords and Commons* (1959), his later anthology *The Golden Treasury of Irish Poetry A.D. 600–1200* (1967),
and his classic study of Irish literature, *The Backward Look*
(1967). The reception which greeted *The Midnight Court*, however, bears witness to the potential dangers of repossession for

Irish writers of the mid-century. It was the object of castigation in the Irish senate for its scurrilous and licentious material, and it was subsequently banned. There can be no clearer testimony to the myopic conservatism of those governmental proponents of an 'Irish Ireland' who could not stomach some of the actual— scandalously licentious—products of that 'hidden Ireland' which they claimed to be bringing once more to light. Seamus Heaney's *The Midnight Verdict* (1993) publishes a version of part of the Merriman poem together with a version of the Orpheus and Eurydice story from Ovid's *Metamorphoses*, giving yet further life in English to the disputatious text.

Kinsella has himself edited the work of another controversial and antagonistic figure of the Irish mid-century, Austin Clarke, whose interest in Gaelic prosody led him to experiment with some of its forms, or versions of some of them, in his English poems. The result is a poetry heavily dependent on systems of assonance, alliteration, and internal rhyme rather than end-rhyme. If this originated in a reverence towards Irish-language prosody and the culture it contains, it was turned towards English expressive possibilities too, since, by a suggestive imitation of these forms, he thought, he would ensure that 'lovely and neglected words are advanced to the tonic place and divide their echoes'.[16] The resulting poems are like nothing else in the language, and if their intricacies occasionally seem contrived, they also at times achieve qualities of musicality exceptional in English, as in the opening stanza of the title poem of *Pilgrimage and Other Poems* (1928) which manages both a hushed dignity and a sinuous, feline movement, a kind of rippling and stalking in metre ('Ara' is Clarke's mythological name for the Aran islands, off the west coast of Ireland):

> When the far south glittered
> Behind the grey beaded plains,
> And cloudier ships were bitted
> Along the pale waves,
> The showery breeze—that plies
> A mile from Ara—stood
> And took our boat on sand:

> There by dim wells the women tied
> A wish on thorn, while rainfall
> Was quiet as the turning of books
> In the holy schools at dawn.

Pilgrimage and Other Poems was published as the government
of the Irish Free State was preparing to introduce its Censorship
of Publications Act in 1929 (from which Clarke was to suffer
regularly in his life as succeeding books were banned), and as
the forces of Catholic reaction were establishing that foothold
which was eventually to lead to the formal recognition of the
'special place' of the Catholic Church in the constitution of
the Irish Republic in 1937. Clarke's view of the Irish tradition
was, like O'Connor's, one that flew in the face of this state
authoritarianism. His effort was to reappropriate a Christianity
more attractively humane, in what he read as its earlier eroticism
and licence, than the Jansenist version of his own upbringing.
The twin historical focuses of his attention in this effort were the
early medieval Ireland of the period he called the 'Celtic-
Romanesque' and the Ireland of the eighteenth century. Like
the re-creation of a historical and legendary Alexandria in the
work of the modern Greek poet C. P. Cavafy, Clarke's Celtic-
Romanesque supplies both erotic consolation and the relief of
exasperation and exacerbation. The figure of the 'straying student', the student for the priesthood tempted to abandon his
studies because of the desires of the flesh, is a recurrent one in
the work; and it is partly a self-representation of Clarke in his
own antagonism, anti-clericalism, and ill-alliance. The poem actually called 'The Straying Student' memorably concludes by
insinuating its eighteenth-century, Penal Law setting into con-
temporary Ireland, 'this land | Where every woman's son | Must
carry his own coffin and believe, | In dread, all that the clergy
teach the young'.

If Clarke's approach to versification seems intimately attuned
to a career of such exemplary and taxing refusals of the conventional and the collusive, it has also been thought by some critics
merely mechanistic. Almost always having an air of some eccen-
tricity, it has had few imitators (but it has had some: notably the

English poet Donald Davie). The more usual way has been for
writers to bring elements of the Gaelic culture more straightforwardly, but still anxiously, into their own modern English.
Michael Hartnett has published volumes of versions of the
eighteenth-century poet O Bruadair and the seventeenth-
century Haicéad, and his own work has nervously hesitated
between Irish and English: his poem 'A Farewell to English'
(which Kinsella placed at the end of his *Oxford Book*) signals a
disgust with various ways of accommodating the Gaelic tradition
in English and makes explicit his decision to move from one
language into the other, a decision since rescinded. John
Montague, in his poem 'The Wild Dog Rose' in *Tides* (1970),
which became the climactic poem of his sequence *The Rough
Field* (1972), a grim narrative of violence and rape, brings a
revised *cailleach* figure into strange and fruitful alliance with a
neo-Wordsworthian contemplation of solitude. Elsewhere, in
poems such as 'Hero's Portion' and 'Heroics', he meditates on
images and emblems drawn from the early medieval Irish period; and he occasionally includes translations from the Irish as
parts of his own meditative poetic sequences, notably the version of an eleventh-century poem which appears as part of 'The
Cave of Night' in *A Slow Dance* (1975). In one of his finest
poems, 'A Grafted Tongue', which eventually found its place in
The Rough Field, he uncovers in the 'ordeal' of his own stammer
an emblem for the profound alienation of that first generation of
Irish-speaking schoolchildren forced to speak English:

> To grow
> a second tongue, as
> harsh a humiliation
> as twice to be born.

Such poems make it plain why Montague observes in one of
his essays that 'An Irishman of Gaelic background is, in a sense,
a White Indian'.[17] The definition may go some way towards
explaining the younger poet Paul Muldoon's interest in Native
American themes. They feature significantly in his work, from
'The Year of the Sloes, for Ishi' in his first book, *New Weather*

(1973), through the lengthy 'The More a Man has the More a Man Wants' in *Quoof* (1983), where the Trickster cycle of the Winnebago Indians is intricately interwoven with an account of an Irish terrorist on the run, to *Madoc* (1990) and the opera libretto *Shining Brow* (1993). Muldoon's work also contains Irish legendary and mythological material just below its guileful postmodern surface, so frequently as to make a handbook of Celtic mythology a prerequisite for its proper understanding. It also occasionally translates directly from the Irish, as in the poem 'Keen' in *Mules* (1977), which is a version of a tiny section of one of the greatest of all poems in Irish, the eighteenth-century *Lament for Art O'Leary* by his wife, Eileen Dubh Ní Chonaill. It is in the long poem 'Immram' in *Why Brownlee Left* (1980), however, that Muldoon offers his most extended, but characteristically playful and metamorphic confrontation with an original Irish source: the eighth-century Irish voyage narrative *Immram Mael Duin*, in which the hero goes in quest of his father's murderer but, on the advice of a hermit, ultimately refuses to exact revenge.

Muldoon's 'Immram' is, like the work of Ní Dhomhnaill, a subversion of the earnestness, and certainly of the conservative nationalist assumptions, of a great deal of earlier translation from the Irish. Muldoon is presumably attracted to the original partly because of the fortuitous similarity of its hero's name to his own ('Mael Duin'/'Muldoon'), and he takes over the basic plot of the dangerous journey, together with a number of images and motifs twisted into parodistic form: a beautiful woman in the original becomes a high-class prostitute; a magical door becomes a revolving hotel door; the white-haired hermit becomes a recluse of the Howard Hughes variety. In 'Immram' these themes and motifs from the ancient Irish wonder-tale are yoked to a jauntily hip pastiche of the mid-century Los Angeles vernacular of Raymond Chandler and to a wanderingly digressive plot of a gumshoe story kind.

It would clearly be beside the point to attempt to interpret the poem too earnestly: its levity of tone and the fun of its discrepant pastiche and exuberant versification make it, on a primary level, as delightfully easy a read as the work of that other excellent contemporary pasticheur of Chandlerian modes, Kinky Friedman. However, it undoubtedly has other purposes in mind too. Muldoon twice situates his hero behind 'Mr. and Mrs. Alfred Tennyson'; and in relation to his source he is himself situated 'behind' the poet Tennyson, who published his own version of *Immram Mael Duin*, as 'The Voyage of Mael Duin', in 1880. That version, according to his son Hallam Tennyson, was intended as 'symbolical of the contest between Roman Catholics and Protestants'.[18] Narratives, Muldoon's strange new 'translation' appears to imply, always come behind others which may well have their own ideological purposes in mind. Similarly, his revision of the original plot into the son's circular, unfinished, and fruitless search for a father, rather than a father's killer, implies the folly of looking for a source of any original purity. The point of the digressive story appears to be that what makes us what we are is the journey or the quest itself, not the point of origin or arrival. 'Immram' offers itself as a celebration of crossed strains and impure pedigrees.

The poem's melding of its pre-existent Irish and American texts may well be, then, a wry and subtle recognition of one of the salient facts of Irish history: the emigration to America of succeeding generations after the Famine of 1845—including, as it happens, some of Raymond Chandler's own forebears. Hence the presence in the Los Angeles Police Department, in Muldoon's poem, of 'Lieutenant Brendan O'Leary', whose own father thinks of the American Irish as 'the Israelites of Europe'—'But he might as well have been Jewish', says O'Leary, with a nonchalance which subverts all reactionary nationalist myths of origin and pure identity. The libertarian implication of this inventive 'translation' would appear to be that originals find their proper place in revisions; that purity is a fascistic idea, in literary as well as in genetic theory.

When John Montague, no doubt partly ironically, claims to be a 'White Indian', he also observes that 'the poet-king Sweeny, who was translated into a bird, might be a figure—Raven, Crow—from Haida legend'.[19] This figure, sometimes spelt

'Sweeney', flits frequently through modern Irish writing. A kind of incarnate translation—at once king, poet, and bird—he may be found briefly in Montague himself, in Ní Dhomnaill, and in Muldoon. He also appears at the very beginning of Austin Clarke's career, in the poem 'The Frenzy of Suibhne', and at its very end, in 'The Trees of the Forest', in a way that suggests that Clarke was, to some extent, reading his own biography through the Sweeney figure. He features most notably, however, in Flann O'Brien's comic and experimental novel *At Swim-Two-Birds* (1939), and in Seamus Heaney's translation *Sweeney Astray* (1983) and his sequence 'Sweeney Redivivus' in the volume *Station Island* (1984). In these works Sweeney becomes a significant mode of self-definition and a compelling self-image for the modern Irish writer.

The Irish text is *Buile Suibhne* (literally 'The Madness of Sweeney'), written in a combination of poetry and prose, which survives in a seventeenth-century manuscript but is thought to have begun taking shape in the ninth century, developing material going back as far as the Battle of Moira in AD 637. Sweeney is a tribal king cursed by the priest Ronan for dishonouring him. The curse transforms Sweeney into a maddened bird-man condemned to fly over Ireland and western Scotland in an unresting, outcast condition, cut off from family, friends, and tribe. Despondent and mistrustful, he lives alone in the wilderness, feeding off berries and watercress, sleeping in the bushes and trees, and pausing every so often in some favourite place, particularly the frequently described Glen Bolcain. After a series of adventures and encounters with such figures as the Hag of the Mill, who enters into a weird leaping contest with him which culminates in her death, and with the madman Alan in Scotland, Sweeney eventually suffers the death long since foretold for him: in the churchyard of the priest Moling he is hit by the spear of a jealous husband, and receives a Christian burial. The text sets descriptions of Sweeney's plight alongside his own complaints at his fate and his vivid and poignant evocations of the landscape he flies over.

One reason for the sustained interest in the story of Sweeney is that it locates as an arresting fiction something permanently relevant to an Irish religious sensibility and consciousness: the dispute or tension between the ancient Celtic and pagan world-view and the new order of monastic Christianity. In Sweeney's rebellion against Ronan and in his eventual uneasy alliance with the cleric Moling we have another version of the antagonism explored elewhere in Irish writing—in Yeats, for instance—as that between Oisin and Patrick. *Buile Suibhne* enacts the drama of culture and conscience—and enacts it as grief—when one way of perceiving the world collapses under the greater power of another. In his 'grammar of poetic myth' *The White Goddess*, however, Robert Graves describes the poem as 'the most ruthless and bitter description in all European literature of an obsessed poet's predicament';[20] and this is undoubtedly a large part of the story's relevance to both O'Brien and Heaney. In the introduction to his translation Heaney observes that 'insofar as Sweeney is . . . a figure of the artist, displaced, guilty, assuaging himself by his utterance, it is possible to read the work as an aspect of the quarrel between free creative imagination and the constraints of religious, political and domestic obligation'. His version of the poem as *Sweeney Astray* (1983) becomes, therefore, a self-involved homage to the Irish text which fixes Sweeney, the 'bare figure of pain', as a permanent feature of English as well as Irish literature.

But Heaney's interest in Sweeney extends beyond the translation itself. In 'Sweeney Redivivus' he 'translates' himself more intimately into Sweeney by, as it were, rhyming some of his own experiences with those of the bird-king. The poem 'The First Flight', for instance, reinvents his controversial move from Belfast to Dublin in 1972 as a version of Sweeney's stubborn refusal to be persuaded from his tree by his relative Lynchseachan. By adopting some of the situations, images, and devices of the medieval text, and by employing also a figurative language drawn from the monastic scriptorium, the sequence deflects some difficult matters of personal biography and creativity into a form which gives such perturbing emotions as pride, disdain, anger, and regret an expression at once both accurate and coded. Stepping, as the first poem in the sequence puts it, 'from a justified line | into the margin', Heaney develops the figure of Sweeney as outlaw and outsider in order to scrutinize newly and unpredictably his relationship with his own origins in a Northern Catholic family and community, with Irish nationalism and Catholicism, with his literary peers and critics, and with the expectations of his audience.

Heaney says in his introduction to *Sweeney Astray* that Flann O'Brien's version of the story is 'as hilarious as it is melancholy'. In fact, the undoubted hilarity of O'Brien's *At Swim-Two-Birds* is not really dependent on the lengthy translation of the Sweeney material which nevertheless figures centrally in the book. That material is, like Heaney's own translation, much more purely melancholy, the product of O'Brien's manifestly admiring desire to render the emotions of the original with accuracy. What makes for the hilarity is actually the way the translated Sweeney material is combined with other less reverently plundered, parodied, and travestied texts, and with a great deal of self-reflexive critical commentary, in this *tour-de-force* of fictive cunning and manipulation whose Chinese-box construction has made it exemplary in some recent accounts of post-modern narrative.

It is almost impossible to describe *At Swim-Two-Birds* without making it sound chaotic; but the sense of chaos being just kept in check by a devotedly, if almost dementedly, systematic imagination is very much part of its effect. The book is heavily influenced by Joyce. Its basic structure is derived from the 'Cyclops' episode of *Ulysses*, whose technique (named 'gigantism' by Joyce) involves the alternation of more-or-less realistic passages, which reproduce conversations in a Dublin pub, with parodies, often very extensive, of various conventions and clichés of Irish writing. In the 'realistic' parts of *At Swim* the book's first, unnamed narrator is an apparently slothful, drunken student at University College Dublin who is neverthe-less writing a novel, and is eventually academically successful. In what seems a mood and tone inherited from the deflationary, satirical Joyce of *Dubliners*, this narrator lives with his uncle, apparently a prime instance of small-minded, cliché-ridden, slyly manipulative lower-middle-class Irish pietism. His misunderstandings of his nephew are a frequent comic resource: 'Tell me this: do you ever open a book at all?' is his constant enquiry of this astonishingly bookish narrator in this most astonishingly bookish of books. Nevertheless, at the end of the novel, when the narrator has made good, his uncle surprises him with an act of spontaneous affection and generosity: 'My luck had evinced unsuspected traits of character and had induced in me an emotion of surprise and contrition extremely difficult of literary rendition or description.'

The sense here that there are some things—and they may be the most significant things—that literature cannot say is probably the impulse behind the novel's numerous parodies, which insist on the presumptuousness of the claims of literature that it can get so many different things said well. O'Brien is a radical sceptic about literary artifice and a malevolent subverter of any secure authorial authority. In *At Swim*, the hero of the student narrator's novel, Trellis, is also writing a novel, although there are strong implications that this novel depends too heavily, even plagiaristically, on the work of another novelist, Tracy. Unfortunately, Trellis suffers from the inability to get out of bed, with the result that his characters—who include that hero of ancient Irish myth, Finn MacCool, and that figure from ersatz Irish legend, the Pooka MacPhellimey—manage to lead lives independent of him and also to tell their own stories. These stories involve a riot of parodies of various originals, ranging from the texts of the Irish Literary Revival to the cowboy westerns of contemporary pulp fiction. Eventually, in these coinciding or colliding fictions, the aptly named Trellis (the structure on which these narratives proliferate) has a son called Orlick, fully grown at the moment of birth, who is, naturally, also a novelist, of a 'high-class' kind; and, directed by others of Trellis's embittered characters, he writes a fiction in order to denigrate and damage his father. This culminates in a trial in which his characters act as both judge and jury of Trellis, and the whole 'story-teller's book-web' ends in a kind of scherzo of even further, unexpected intertextual reference before the manuscript is burnt by a maid.

Some of the book's most notable parodies are the sections concerning Finn MacCool, and it is during one of these that Finn himself tells the story of Sweeney or, as O'Brien has it, 'Sweeny'. There is a sense in which, once introduced, he takes over the whole narrative: since, after Finn has told his story, with numerous interruptions from the other characters, Sweeny is pulled out of his tale into theirs by becoming the object of their tender solicitude in a luminous and hallucinatory episode which is in many ways the heart of the book. Carried in procession through the dark, singing his laments, Sweeny comes to act as a poignant parallel for the more farcical fate of the author Trellis who, outcast and condemned by his own characters, also takes to the trees. Against some of the book's parodies, which render the euphemisms, periphrases, banalities, and bathos of some typical kinds of Irish translation with a merciless accuracy of subversive mimicry, and against the preposterous and self-serving chauvinism of Trellis himself (who, for instance, will read only books with green covers), the Sweeney material proposes an alternative model of intelligent and scrupulous translation. In O'Brien Sweeney becomes thereby the representative figure for a genuine pathos or even tragedy in some types of Irish historical experience, recoverable by devoted acts of translation. He is the outlaw forced to take to the woods; the poet whose truth-telling is reviled by his people; and even, when his mouth is described as stained green by the watercress he feeds off, the victim of starvation and famine. Although O'Brien's Sweeny eventually ends up reductively playing poker in the back room of a Dublin pub, *At Swim-Two-Birds* still exists in an atmosphere of mournfulness and repining which undermines its comic hyperbole: 'There was a gentle rustle in the thick of the green branches, a slow caress like the visit of a summer breeze in a field of oats, a faint lifeless movement: and a voice descended on the travellers, querulous and saddened with an infinite weariness.'

Appearing like this in the frenzy of *At Swim-Two-Birds*, Sweeney makes it clear why he has since figured in one further unpredictable metamorphosis in modern Irish writing. When Brian Keenan, the Belfast hostage, began composing poetry in his Beirut captivity, he tells us in the remarkable account of his ordeal, *An Evil Cradling* (1992), it seemed to him that the poetry was written by someone else: 'I could hardly bear to see, not so much the words themselves, but the man who had put them there: Mad Sweeney hiding in his tree of words.' Keenan's identification with the figure offers yet further testimony to Sweeney's ability both to express and to offer some palliation for emotions of terror, subjection, and desire. Even under the almost insupportable duress of the hostage's cell Sweeney acts too as an emblem for the frenzy or madness of writing itself, for its double weave of entrapment and escape.

4. Dead Language: Samuel Beckett

At the end of *Ulysses* Joyce appends the places and dates of its composition in a way that was then startlingly original for a literary work, although it has been much imitated since: '*Trieste–Zürich–Paris*, 1914–1921.' In doing so, he is making it clear that this work about Dublin in 1904 was the product of lengthy gestation and composition away from Dublin, in a number of famous European cities. Joyce's dissatisfaction with the repressions of British imperial Dublin, and with many of the proposed nationalist alternatives to it, involved his lifelong voluntary exile from Ireland. Exile may be thought a form of self-translation, in which you move yourself into a different country and culture and, often, take on the necessity of speaking a different language. Flann O'Brien was extremely loath to admit the Joycean influence on him; and one of his difficulties with Joyce was that he felt himself, as a stay-at-home Dublin civil servant, inevitably conformist-seeming in comparison with the implicitly heroic Joycean example. As Anthony Cronin's biography of O'Brien makes plain, the life of intellectual and artistic Dublin between the 1930s and 1960s could be a deeply dispiriting and disabling one: there were few writers of that period not in some way maimed by it.[21] Self-imposed exile, on the Joycean model, was an obvious and available alternative for such mid-century Irish modernist poets as Brian Coffey and Denis Devlin, who produced their work outside Ireland. But only Samuel Beckett, who followed Joyce into Parisian exile and came to know him well, took the concept of translation so far as to begin to write, in the 1950s, in the foreign language itself—French—and then to translate himself into English. The result is one of the strangest and strongest individual bodies of work in modern Irish literature.

The relative placelessness of Beckett's major texts and the peculiar kinds of English derived from what he calls 'the wastes and wilds of self-translation' have tended to occlude what is specifically Irish in his work. Some recent scholarship, however, notably Eoin O'Brien's *The Beckett Country* (1986) and John P. Harrington's *The Irish Beckett* (1991), have done much to restore a context which places Beckett illuminatingly in relation to his origins, which may in some ways be thought to plot a trajectory for much of his later work. His earliest writings, including the collection of interrelated stories *More Pricks Than Kicks* (1934), and his first two novels, *Murphy* (1938) and *Watt* (1953, but written in 1945), and also his critical writings of the 1930s collected in the volume *Disjecta* (1983), contain a critique of the post-revolutionary Irish Free State all the more savage for its cold and controlled disdain. The targets of Beckett's fastidiously mordant hostility include, prominently, the statutes outlawing contraception and the Censorship Act, whose lists of unpermitted texts included his own, needless to say.

In *Watt* the attack focuses on the banning of the fictional product 'Bando': 'For the State, taking as usual the law into its own hands, and duly indifferent to the sufferings of thousands of men, and tens of thousands of women, all over the country, has seen fit to place an embargo on the admirable article, from which joy would stream, at a moderate cost, into homes, and other places of rendezvous, now desolate.' If this deadpan passage implies in one precise way why the narrow-minded pietism and repressiveness of this legislating state might well drive this author into voluntary exile, it may also suggest a reason why images of desolation and dereliction are so prominent in his

subsequent work. This early passage referring to an actual Irish
social situation manifests exactly that combination of a punctili-
ously elegant, deflationary syntax and style and a reduced dilapidation of circumstance which are to remain one of Beckett's
uniquely characteristic signatures. The passage is complemented
by a very striking interruption to the later story *First Love* (1973)
which, with a quite exceptional explicitness, sets a larger context
for that desolation:

What constitutes the charm of our country, apart of course from its
scant population, and this without help of the meanest contraceptive, is
that all is derelict, with the sole exception of history's ancient faeces.
These are ardently sought after, stuffed and carried in procession.
Wherever nauseated time has dropped a nice fat turd you will find our
patriots, sniffing it up on all fours, their faces on fire. Elysium of the
roofless. Hence my happiness at last. Lie down, all seems to say, lie
down and stay down.[22]

The scatology of this is almost Swiftian, as it offers a figure for
the way a past can become dangerously fossilized, the hopeless
recourse of a people left 'roofless' not only by the politics of the
colonial power which has withdrawn, but also by the repressive
measures of the post-colonial state itself, which prevents contraception without taking up the necessary consequential responsibility of supplying roof or opportunity.

In this passage the motivation for Beckett's own voluntary
exile coincides with the hopelessness which leads to emigration.
Its discursive explicitness may offer some historical and political,
as opposed to the more usual psychological and metaphysical,
contexts for all those figures of moribund stasis in the work: Nag
and Nell in their dustbins and Hamm in his wheelchair in *End-
game* (1957); Winny up to her neck in sand in *Happy Days*
(1961); the characters in their urns in *Play* (1963); the bedridden
Malone in *Malone Dies* (1951); Vladimir and Estragon abjectly
but ungainsayably incapable of motion at the end of *Waiting for
Godot* (1953).

If the passage from *First Love* is unusually explicit, references
to Irish nationalist history do nevertheless murmur unexpectedly elsewhere in Beckett too (the Battle of Aughrim and

the death of the Republican Noel Lemass in *Mercier and Camier* (1970), and the hunger-strike of Terence MacSwiney, Lord Mayor of Cork, in *Malone Dies*). In the earlier work Beckett is also caustic about some of the effects of what he reads as a literary and cultural nationalism. In *Murphy* Austin Clarke is pilloried as the 'pot poet' Austin Ticklepenny, who writes 'the class of pentameter [he] felt it his duty to Erin to compose' and is incarcerated in a lunatic asylum. (The satire here is cruelly unyielding, since Clarke did himself spend time in a mental hospital, the experience which he eventually turned to poetic profit in his long poem 'Mnemosyne Lay in Dust' (1966)). It is a gas contraption set up by Ticklepenny which eventually explodes and kills the novel's eponymous hero. Murphy, blown up by the gas of the Dublin pot poet, then undergoes a macabre inspection in the morgue: 'Neary saw Clonmacnois on the slab, the castle of the O'Melaglins, meadow, eskers, thatch on white, something red, the wide bright water, Connaught.' When these names resonant in nationalist mythology, accompanied by an imagery derived both from that mythology and from the advertisements of the Irish tourist industry, are all read bizarrely out of an exploded corpse, they make the novel's concluding stab at the pretentions of those Beckett calls the 'twilighters' in his acerbic essay 'Recent Irish Poetry' (1934). They are at one in their venom with the novel's earlier description of this same Neary dashing his head against the buttocks—'such as they are'—of the heroic statue of Cuchulain in the Dublin General Post Office, erected to commemorate the Easter Rising of 1916. It is a moment in which Beckett makes recognitions similar to those made by Joyce at the end of the 'Sirens' episode of *Ulysses*, where the tremendous final words from the dock of the condemned nationalist hero Robert Emmet are drowned out by Leopold Bloom's thunderous fart.

Beckett is on record as saying that his decision to write in French was because 'en français c'est plus facile d'écrire sans style' ('in French it is easier to write without style').[23] In a letter written to an acquaintance, Axel Kaun, in 1937, he offers an uncharacteristically explicit statement of his extreme linguistic self-consciousness:

It is indeed becoming more and more difficult, even senseless, for me to write an official English. And more and more my own language appears to me like a veil that must be torn apart in order to get at the things (or the Nothingness) behind it. Grammar and Style. To me they have become as irrelevant as a Victorian bathing suit or the imperturbability of a true gentleman. A mask. Let us hope that the time will come, thank God that in certain circles it has already come, when language is most efficiently used where it is being most efficiently misused. As we cannot eliminate language all at once, we should at least leave nothing undone that might contribute to its falling into disrepute. To bore one hole after another in it, until what lurks behind it—be it something or nothing—begins to seep through; I cannot imagine a higher goal for a writer today.[24]

If this reveals the not-uncommon radicalism and experimentalism of a young writer self-consciously allying himself with the first generation of European modernists, it also allows itself to be read as the specific alienation from an 'official English' of a writer who is not nationally English but who also, given the anti-nationalist orientations of his earlier work, wishes to avoid the suspect signals given out by the use of Hiberno-English. The move from English to French is the clearest possible exhibition of Beckett's opting for an attempted traditionlessness in his writing. The empty stasis of *Waiting for Godot*, in particular, seems almost a pantomime of the lack of a sustaining tradition. In this sense, Beckett's language of exhaustion and abjection may almost envy the condition of that language actually largely 'eliminated' and 'fallen into disrepute', Irish.

The language is referred to several times in the work, notably in the radio play *All That Fall* (1957), which was, exceptionally for Beckett after the 1950s, written in English and, also exceptionally, with a specifically, if fictionally, Irish setting:

MR ROONEY: Do you know, Maddy, sometimes one would think you were struggling with a dead language.

MRS ROONEY: Yes, indeed, Dan, I know full well what you mean, I
  often have that feeling, it is unspeakably excruciating.
MR ROONEY: I confess I have it sometimes myself, when I happen to
  overhear what I am saying.
MRS ROONEY: Well, you know, it will be dead in time, just like our own
  poor dear Gaelic, there is that to be said.
[*Urgent baa.*]

'Tears and laughter, they are so much Gaelic to me', says
Molloy, morosely; and the sad futility of this linguistic dissolution may also act as a figure for Beckett's despair of the referential properties of all language. 'It seemed to me that all language
was an excess of language', says the again eminently quotable
Molloy.

In fact, even when Beckett translates himself into English out
of French there persists, wistfully, the presence of Hiberno-
English forms and idioms: in *Godot*, for instance, we have such
intermittent tendernesses as 'Go and see is he hurt', 'Was I long
asleep?', and 'Get up till I embrace you'. In these expressions we
hear Vladimir and Estragon actually struggling with the dead
language of 'Gaelic', which obtrudes its syntax and idiom into
their English. And, to compound the Beckettian reflexivity, that
English is itself formed by the 'death' of the French language out
of which it has been translated. The later Beckettian language,
refined distillate of Hiberno-English and French, is undoubtedly
testimony to the anti-nationalist and even anti-national view of
art he expresses in a note on Jack B. Yeats—'The artist who
stakes his being is from nowhere, has no kith'[25]—but it equally
supports such opposed statements from the texts themselves as
that towards the end of *The Unnamable* (1959)—'I'm on the
island, I've never left the island, God help me'—and one of the
'addenda' to *Watt*—'for all the good that frequent departures
out of Ireland had done him, he might just as well have stayed
there.'

Beckett's language is also, however, a strategy for coping with
what might well otherwise have been the overwhelming and
stultifying influence of Joyce. Apparently acting for a while in a
secretarial capacity for Joyce, and enduring a complex entangle-

ment with his daughter Lucia, Beckett had a difficult personal relationship with the older writer, who wished him to behave at times, it seems, as a surrogate son.[26] In literary terms, Beckett's decision to write in French may be regarded as an overcoming of his initial willing filiality by the most fundamental act of disobedience. The estrangement from Joyce became possible only in the profound act of self-estrangement that is involved in writing a language not your mother—or your father—tongue.

There are several parodistic allusions to Joyce in Beckett. The rain that falls in the story 'A Wet Night' in *More Pricks Than Kicks*—'It fell upon the bay, the littoral, the mountains and the plains, and notably upon the Central Bog it fell with a rather desolate uniformity'—remembers the rather purple cadences of the snow at the end of 'The Dead' in *Dubliners*; Krapp's memory of his love affair in *Krapp's Last Tape* (1958) echoes Bloom's memories of Molly's first kiss in the 'Lestrygonians' episode of *Ulysses*; and a passage in *How It Is* (1964) travesties Molly Bloom's final soliloquy: her famous 'yes I said yes I will Yes', which is frequently read as deeply and comically affirmative, becomes the Beckettian hero's wretchedly disgusted 'yes all balls yes'. But it is in a brief allegorical passage of *Molloy*, the first published of his French writings, that Beckett gives the relationship its most generous, if coded, acknowledgement. These punning lines, with their allusions to the titles of Joyce's two un-ignorable books, *Ulysses* and *Finnegans Wake*, and to Joyce's own name, express both the deep indebtedness and the necessary divorce, as Beckett definitively translates himself out of the Joycean sphere of influence ('Geulincx' here is the seventeenth-century Belgian follower of Descartes who fascinated Beckett early in his career):

I who had loved the image of old Geulincx, dead young, who left me free, on the black boat of Ulysses, to crawl towards the East, along the deck. That is a great measure of freedom, for him who has not the pioneering spirit. And from the poop, poring upon the wave, a sadly rejoicing slave, I follow with my eyes the proud and futile wake. Which, as it bears me from no fatherland away, bears me onward to no shipwreck.

2

A Slight Inflection: Representations
of the Big House

> It has set, simply, its pattern of trees and avenues on the
> virgin, anonymous countryside. Like Flaubert's ideal book
> about nothing, it sustains itself on itself by the inner force
> of its style.
>
> (Elizabeth Bowen, *Bowen's Court*)

> In most cases these houses maintained no culture worth
> speaking of—nothing but an absolute bravado, an insidious
> bonhomie and a way with horses.
>
> (Louis MacNeice, *The Poetry of W. B. Yeats*)

1. Pathos and Pollution: W. B. Yeats

The literature of the Irish 'Big House'—of, that is, the social and
cultural organization of the Anglo-Irish or Protestant Ascendancy class in their houses and on their estates or 'demesnes'—
extends from Maria Edgeworth's *Castle Rackrent*, published
in 1800, to contemporary fictions such as those of Jennifer
Johnston and John Banville.[1] A significant sub-genre in Irish
writing, it is predominantly a novelistic tradition. However, one
of its most important manifestations in the modern period, to
which other texts make reference, is the poetry of Yeats. He
engages with themes, motifs, or images drawn from the Big
House throughout his career; and, in a range of work including
'Upon a House Shaken by the Land Agitation' in *The Green
Helmet* (1910), 'Ancestral Houses' in *The Tower* (1928), the
twinned 'Coole Park, 1929' and 'Coole and Ballylee, 1931' in
The Winding Stair (1933), and the deeply problematic and embittered late play *Purgatory* (1939), it becomes a dominant and

organizing preoccupation, a nucleus about which some of his most besetting ideas and emotions hover.

Coole Park in Co. Galway, where Yeats spent much of his time under the patronage of Lady Augusta Gregory, is the major scene of celebration. He defines Coole as a centre of both 'traditional' value—which he associates with what he considered, or partly invented, as the cultural high point of the Anglo-Irish eighteenth century—and of current intellectual and civic distinction, a numinous meeting place 'Where passion and precision have been one | Time out of mind', as 'Upon a House Shaken by the Land Agitation' puts it. Under the organizational brilliance of Lady Gregory, the benefits of a venerable cultural heritage— 'Where wings have memory of wings, and all | That comes of the best knit to the best'—are made available to those capable of transmitting them to the needful future. What gives these poems their distinction, however, the thing sounded in their elegiac cadences, is not only the almost Renaissance glamour of the celebration but the consciousness of loss: since for Yeats the history of modern Ireland is the turning away from the gracious civilization represented by houses such as Coole towards that despised and feared *petit-bourgeois* culture which 'September 1913' characterizes as formed by those who 'fumble in a greasy till'. Hence the possession of Yeats's imagination by anticipations of Coole's destruction, when, for instance, he evokes the desolation of its absence—'When nettles wave upon a shapeless mound'—in 'Coole Park, 1929', which was actually written several years before the house was in fact razed to the ground in 1932.

In these poems Yeats is crystallizing a complex of Anglo-Irish anxieties. The Wyndham Act of 1903 and later Land Acts in 1909 and 1910—those which lie behind 'Upon a House Shaken by the Land Agitation'—confirmed what had already long been clear: that the political power of the Anglo-Irish was to become much reduced as a result of falling revenues from their estates. When, after the War of Independence, the Civil War, and the establishment of the Irish Free State in the early 1920s, it finally became plain to Yeats that his dream of an Ireland uniting its best Irish and Anglo-Irish traditions was never to be realized, his reaction was a deep disquiet and ultimate gloomy embitterment. In 'Ancestral Houses', written just before the Civil War, but published as part of the sequence 'Meditations in Time of Civil War' in *The Tower* (1928), this is reflected in an anxiety that the elegant, eighteenth-century grace of the Big House and its gardens may have made its inheritors passive and inert. Spoilt, as it were, by the highest achievement of their own class, the current possessors of these houses may lack the capacity for the 'violence' and 'bitterness' necessary to sustain their authority. In *Purgatory*, more despairingly, this becomes a disgust at the collusion of a class in its own disintegration. The play's grim plot concerns an old man, the son of a Big House, who has murdered his father, considering him responsible for the house's ruination because he has come from outside the class of the Anglo-Irish. During the play this old man murders his son too, in order to prevent further 'pollution' of their lineage. He also witnesses the moment of his own conception in the supernatural Big House which is the site of the play's 'Purgatory', since his mother is condemned to spend her afterlife repeating the shame and remorse of the act which brought about the house's downfall. *Purgatory* is in many respects a revolting play, the dark underside and hysterical extreme of the regretful plangencies of some of the poems.

In 'The Literary Myths of the Revival', an influential essay, Seamus Deane has written of the significant place of Yeats's conception of the Big House in the Irish novelistic tradition.[2] He sees the central Yeatsian themes of Romantic nostalgia and the pathos of ruin maintaining a suspect afterlife in those numerous novels of the Big House which followed on the collapse of the social organization of Anglo-Irish life in the 1920s. Such novels would include Elizabeth Bowen's *The Last September* (1929), Molly Keane's greatly under-rated earlier novels (published under the pseudonym M. J. Farrell), *Mad Puppetstown* (1931) and *Two Days in Aragon* (1941), Jennifer Johnston's *The Old Jest* (1979) and *Fool's Sanctuary* (1987), William Trevor's *Fools of Fortune* (1983), J. G. Farrell's *Troubles* (1970), and John Banville's *Birchwood* (1973).

In addition to these historical novels set in the 1920s, at the moment of crisis and disintegration, the 'Big House' theme is prominent elsewhere in modern Irish fiction too: in the late Somerville and Ross novel, *The Big House of Inver* (1925), a radical, and feminist, critique from within of the disintegration of the Anglo-Irish and also of the violence of their origins (the motto of the Prendevilles of Inver is 'Je Prends', 'I Take'); in almost all of Molly Keane's novels, from the earlier brittle but acidic *Devoted Ladies* (1934) and *Full House* (1935) to the ironic late comedy of *Good Behaviour* (1981) and *Time After Time* (1983); in Aidan Higgins's *Langrishe,Go Down* (1966), set in the 1930s but rich in historical allusion; in the English writer Henry Green's *Loving* (1945), a wittily erotic and inventive turning of the genre on its head, almost literally, with the usual Big House aristocratic plot displaced onto the servants belowstairs, who are all English but in Irish exile during the Second World War; and in Jennifer Johnston's *The Captains and the Kings* (1972), *The Gates* (1973), and *How Many Miles to Babylon?* (1974).

Reading such novels as in various ways servile to Yeats's reactionary celebration of the Big House, Deane regards the tradition itself as an enfeeblement, the manifestation of a lack of resourcefulness and an entrapment in outworn modes, conventions, and images: 'the Big House surrounded by the unruly tenantry, Culture besieged by barbarity, a refined aristocracy beset by a vulgar middle class.'[3] Although some of these fictions may merit some of these terms, the tradition of Big House fiction after Yeats is actually varied and buoyant in ways that such criticism fails to recognize, and its attitudes to class, in particular, are, like some of the Southern fiction of the United States, far less caricaturedly clear-cut and self-assured than might be expected. More self-divided and much less intimately indebted to Yeats than Deane thinks, many of these novels in fact offer a resourceful renovation, interrogation, or subversion of the conventional images and emblems, frequently making of them a critique of Anglo-Irish customs and establishments, and occasionally proposing alternative and newly enabling forms of organization and interrelationship.[4]

2. *Modern Castlerackrents*

Deane is clearly right, however, to emphasize the repetitive nature of the themes and images themselves. An element of pastiche was inherent in the genre from the beginning: Charles Maturin, within a decade of *Castle Rackrent*, was already employing the generic term 'castlerackrents' to describe the novels published in its wake. In modern examples, the reader quickly comes to recognize the common properties. The Big House is in decline, its former glory acting as an ironic measure of present disgrace; and its glory days are usually located where Yeats located them, in the eighteenth century of Grattan and Burke. The fall of the house is frequently a matter of literal, physical depredation. In *The Big House of Inver*, with the estate sold and the house's roof gone, the family is reduced to inhabiting its original Norman tower. The plot of Johnston's *The Gates* turns on the efforts of a wealthy Irish-American family to purchase, as an expensive tourist souvenir, the disused and rusted gates of the Big House in the area their forebears came from. In J. G. Farrell's *Troubles*, the Gothic potential of ruin is realized when the novel's Majestic Hotel becomes a virtually surreal nightmare of uncontrolled vegetal growth and the unhindered breeding of an army of wild cats.

This physical fall from grace is the outward sign of an inward catastrophe, in which what Elizabeth Bowen in her story 'Sunday Afternoon' calls 'the aesthetic of living' has dilapidated into ennui, marital unhappiness, alcoholism, insanity, and domestic treachery. The contrast between a glorious, if fantasized, past and a diminished present is sometimes figured as the sensation of being blamed by the house's ancestral portraits; and this occasionally includes—notably in *The Big House of Inver*, in Elizabeth Bowen's Irish stories, and in Molly Keane's *Mad Puppetstown*—the appearance of actual ghosts. Houses 'never forget', says Keane in that novel; 'What are ghosts but the remembrances they shelter?' She then makes a satirical and political point out of the ability of Easter Chevington, her Irish heroine, to recognize the unhappy ghosts of an English house. The recognition, managed quite without feyness, is the impulsion of Easter's return to Ireland and of her attempt at a more successful accommodation of Anglo-Irish ways to the new compunctions of post-revolutionary Ireland. It is one remarkable instance of a conventional property of the genre being worked into new significance.

Along with the occasional appearance of ghosts, these novels far more frequently tend to personify the house itself. In Bowen's *The Last September*, for instance, Danielstown 'stares' at people and is 'executed' by the IRA. When Stella, the heroine of *The Heat of the Day* (1948), Bowen's novel of the Second World War, visits the Irish house Mount Morris, the encounter of woman and house is evoked in those terms of implicit but tremulous eroticism not uncommon in relationships between women in Bowen's novels ('the house devoted the whole muted fervour of its being to a long gaze'). In Keane, Puppetstown is 'a lonely, wicked old woman of a house' and Aragon is 'like an elegant woman'. Such metaphors and similes dramatize the fact that in these novels rights of property and inheritance, and the kinds of attachment which develop from such rights, are as emotionally compelling as personal and even sexual relationships. They are therefore continuous with the usual major plot impulsion of the books: placing the personal life in the context of public, political event, the Big House novel is always a love story too, of however thwarted, perverse, or incestuous a kind (such as Shibby Pindy's consuming, and disguisedly maternal, love for her half-brother Kit in *The Big House of Inver*).

The representation of the Big House as a woman is complemented, in some novels by women writers—and this is a genre predominantly inhabited by women—with strong and distinct female characterizations. Notable among such figures are the young, relatively callow and inexperienced woman, or *ingénue*, who possesses an artistic or literary sensibility; and, at the other extreme, the figure of the cruel or sadistic mother, or surrogate mother. The literary *ingénues* include Lois in *The Last September*, Easter in *Mad Puppetstown*, Minnie in *The Gates*, and Nancy in Johnston's *The Old Jest*; and the subtle deployment of this figure lends Big House novels such as these some of the attributes of the modern womanly *Bildungsroman* or *Kunstlerroman*, whose major instance in English writing of the period is Dorothy Richardson's *Pilgrimage*. They also enable, outstandingly in Molly Keane, a sometimes damning critique of the philistinism of the usual Big House, and of the corruption of a once noble 'aesthetic of living' into an ethos of venality and mercenariness.

The figure of the cruel mother is one of the most remarkable features of the genre, providing a series of terrifying characterizations of emotional deprivation, sexual loneliness and lack, arrogant presumption, and sadistic domestic relationship. Lady Myra Naylor in *The Last September* is a relatively restrained version; Molly Keane includes one as virtually a staple in almost all of her books, from Lady Olivia Bird in *Full House*, through Nan Foley in *Two Days in Aragon*, to the mother in *Good Behaviour*; and Jennifer Johnston similarly has sons subject to such mothers in *The Captains and the Kings*, where the subjection is shown to have lasted into the son's old age, and in *How Many Miles to Babylon?* The disastrous impact of such figures makes the Big House novel the location of extremes of despotic emotional cruelty: to servants, governesses, penurious family hangers-on, and children (the miseries of the neglected nursery and the bullied weak child are evoked in the genre in a way equalled elsewhere only in the Victorian fictions of Dickens and Charlotte Brontë).

If such characterizations are conventions of the genre, however, they are put through remarkable variations. Myra in *The Last September* may be a relatively mild version of the figure but, in her manipulative domination of her niece Lois, her snobbishly autocratic presumption that she can organize another's emotional life, she is nevertheless the agent of suffocating inhibition for the developing younger woman, a later version of Jane

Austen's Lady Catherine de Burgh in *Pride and Prejudice*, but unlikely to meet in the uncertain Lois the spirited opposition of an Elizabeth Bennet. Molly Keane's Lady Olivia Bird in *Full House* supplies one of the most extreme moments in the history of these figures when, at the climax of havoc wreaked by her cavalier and reflex sadism, she diverts the very possibility of guilt into yet another decorously cultivated act of flower-arranging. In *Good Behaviour*, the first-person narrative of the monstrous daughter Aroon becomes the vehicle for the reader's sympathetic understanding of how she has been made monstrous, precisely, by her mother's monstrosity; it is the book's blackest irony that Aroon, 'the changeless me, the truly unwanted person', is actually 'behaving well' according to the lights of the perverse tradition she has inherited from her mother.

Henry Green, alert in *Loving* to this as to many other characteristics of the genre, portrays in Mrs Tennant a very subtle variant on the figure when, by the merest intimation and innuendo, he implies that, apparently unsuspecting and solicitous, she in fact cruelly pleasures herself in her daughter-in-law's guilty discomfiture about her adultery. But the most complex and challenging of these figures is probably Shibby Pindy in *The Big House of Inver*. A study in the psychopathology of interiorized guilt about illegitimacy, she brings about, through her self-disgust and self-hatred, the destruction of the thing she loves when, through her own agency, Inver is burnt to the ground. In this Hardyesque account of 'the invisible, invincible webs of heredity', the Anglo-Irish house destroyed by fire from within enters into a dark consonance with all of those burnt from without during the War of Independence and the Civil War in the 1920s: between 6 December 1921 and 22 March 1923 192 Big Houses were burnt by incendiaries.[5] The persistence of the psychological after-effects of these conflagrations is sensitively delineated in the fiction of Colm Toibin: in *The South* (1990), his heroine, Katherine Procter, is the uncomprehending daughter of a destroyed house still haunted by its burning, even in the Spain of the 1950s; and in *The Heather Blazing* (1992), the hero, Eamon Redmond, a respectable judge, comes from a Republican family responsible for some of the burnings themselves.

The mother in a position of domestic dominance reflects a social reality of Big House life after the First World War, when husbands and heirs failed to return or returned maimed physically, mentally, or emotionally; and in the novels, the figure of the cruel mother is often complemented by the dead, absent, or ineffectual husband and, occasionally, by the mentally distressed son. The figure also, however, manifests and emblematizes a tradition in decay. The withdrawal of class or caste power is represented by the vanished patriarch; and the vacuum of authority is filled by the flailing, destructive, and self-destructive perversion of maternal affection, when the hitherto repressed women of the House, themselves victims of various kinds of emotional deprivation, assert authority in imitation of the only, despotic ways they know. When these figures become the repository of Anglo-Irish tradition, handing on misery to their children, the whole idea of inheritance becomes inherently contaminated and unstable, 'the aesthetic of living' corrupted into the hollow shams of 'good behaviour'. In these appalling figures of maternal perversion we are given images for Anglo-Ireland in its decline corresponding to the image for colonial Catholic Ireland which Joyce famously finds in *A Portrait of the Artist as a Young Man*: 'the old sow that eats her farrow.'

Such figures and motifs, therefore, signify the ways in which the Big House as a social formation has outstayed its proper historical moment, and knows it; and this is why it is frequently fictionally represented in forms analogous to the representations of the Russian aristocracy and *haute bourgeoisie* before the Revolution in the work of Turgenev and Chekhov (and it is very much *apropos* that modern Irish writers such as Brian Friel and Frank McGuinness have translated these writers). The ending of the political power of the Big House and the effective ending of its cultural significance in the early 1920s also have analogies with the fate of Anglo-India. This is a recognition made by J. G. Farrell when he writes *Troubles* as the first volume of an imperial trilogy which also includes *The Siege of Krishnapur*, a novel of nineteenth-century India, and again when he fills the hotel in *Troubles* with old Anglo-Indian ladies; and made by Polly Devlin too in one of her several perceptive essays on Molly Keane, when she refers to her books as presentations of 'the minutiae of the last days of the Irish Raj'.[6] This coincidence of imperial attitudes becomes briefly explicit in *The Big House of Inver* when the English *parvenu* Burgrave is reminded by an Irish race meeting of his experience of the 'natives' in the West Indies, and when, in his casual racism, he perceives the character Maggie Connor, whose maltreatment eventually culminates in suicide, as a 'negro slave'. It is a sharply satirical moment deriving from the same ironic recognitions made by David Thomson in *Woodbrook* (1974), a Big House text which is not fiction but a beguiling combination of autobiographical memoir and sympathetic, politically sensitive social history, remembering from a long distance the author's time as tutor in a Big House in the West of Ireland in the 1930s:

Like Africans under European rule, the Irish people had lived apart for generations. In some ways they were more detached from their rulers than the people of Africa were. Their social customs, dances, games, the stories they enjoyed, their food, furniture, sex-life did not even arouse the curiosity of anthropologists. Only their music was noticed. By nature, they lack the spontaneity of African people, the free expression of emotion, and centuries of poverty and subjection have made them cautious.[7]

One of the classic satirical figurings of such 'apartness' in the English novel is E. M. Forster's in *A Passage to India*, where Mrs Turton refuses to learn Urdu in anything other than the imperative mood, that being entirely adequate to all her communications with the natives. In a similar way, the relative silence of those beyond the gates in the Big House novel is satirized by Henry Green in *Loving*, where the only Irish character, Paddy O'Conor, the lampman, never speaks directly. His 'sibilants and gutturals' are translated by the maid, Kate, for whom he is the source of erotic as well as linguistic fascination. In other novels too the alienation from those beyond the gates is the source of at least as much fascination and desire as it is of anxiety and insecurity. The theme of problematic and dangerous interconnections between Anglo-Irish and Irish—financial, intellectual, fraternal, and sexual—is in fact the basis of plot in a large number of these fictions, notably *The Big House of Inver*, where Shibby is the illegitimate, and Catholic, daughter of the House who attempts to arrange a marriage between its heir, her half-brother Kit, and the daughter of a wealthy local Catholic land agent, so that the House may be preserved. Although her arrangements end in tragic failure, they have clear political implications for the new Ireland that the book was entering on its publication in 1925.

Such interconnections also control the plots of almost all of Jennifer Johnston's Big House novels, in which good intentions, tolerance, affection, and sympathy are devastatingly thwarted by constricting forms of social, cultural, political, and religious intolerance. The culmination of such relationships is usually the disaster of violent death. This pessimistic sense of the potential for disintegrative and destructive interrelationship is most memorably explored in her novel of the First World War, *How Many Miles to Babylon?*, where the Big House officer, Alec Moore, shoots, as an act of mercy, his childhood friend, the private soldier and Republican Jerry Crowe, who has been sentenced to death for desertion. In this mercy-killing Alec is ensuring his own execution too. The implicitly homo-erotic relationship between the two men, who have spent a night chastely in bed together, is not unique in Johnston's handling of the theme of perilous interconnection. Here, it makes the act of killing an act of love too, and very poignantly joins together the polarities of terror and desire. The political irony of the relationship in *How Many Miles to Babylon?* is that Jerry is fighting for the British Army in order to prepare himself for membership of the IRA. Had he survived the war, he would have been dedicated to Alec's destruction. In shooting Jerry before he can be executed by British troops, Alec might be regarded as saving him from what was to be the fate of the Republican leaders of the Easter Rising in 1916. The irony is complemented by the fact that Jerry dies singing one of the best-known of all rebel songs, 'The Croppy Boy'.

The relationship between the Anglo-Irish and those who live outside the walls of their demesnes is also a focus of attention and anxiety in Elizabeth Bowen's non-fictional prose, which forms a significant social history of the Big House. In the essay called 'The Big House' (1940), she employs a revealing personifying figure for the House's isolation from the ordinary life of the country it inhabits: 'in its silence,' she writes, 'it seems to be contemplating the swell and fall of its own lawns.'[8] The self-reflexivity of this is continuous with the English seventeenth-century country-house poetry of Andrew Marvell; but its seductive hush of reverence, its trance of delighted possession and self-possession, is immediately noticed and castigated in the same essay when Bowen wonders how the houses got 'their "big" name': 'have they been called "big" with a slight inflection—that of hostility, irony?'[9] The narcissism of self-regard, that is to say, is rudely interrupted by the outsider; and it is the outsider who presumes to offer the House the name by which it is known. Defining 'hostility' as only a 'slight inflection', Bowen is revealed flinching from the recognition in the very act of making it.

In those novels of the 'Troubles' in the 1920s in which the anxiety and insecurity are greatly exacerbated by immediate physical danger, the hostility is manifest, as the houses—easy targets of Republican detestation—are burnt down in terrorist attacks. *The Last September* is, as its title implies, shadowed by the sense of an ending: the book witnesses the end of a house; of frail human relationships and bodies; and of a powerful social class. Its inertia and ennui derive from what the most sensitive—indeed, almost tremblingly alert—characters, Lois and her cousin Laurence, consider their own superfluity, perceiving themselves part of 'a prologue being played out too lengthily, with unnecessary stress . . . while, unapproachably elsewhere, something went by without them'. That 'something', which is the process of a history in which they have no part, is very interestingly imaged, in this book much given to images of perception (Lois is a painter), as a different kind of contemplation altogether from the House's self-contemplation in Bowen's 'Big House' essay:

A sense of exposure, of being offered without resistance to some ironic uncuriosity, made Laurence look up at the mountain over the roof of the house. In some gaze—of a man's up there hiding, watching among the clefts and ridges—they seemed held, included and to have their only being. The sense of a watcher, reserve of energy and intention, abashed Laurence, who turned from the mountain. But the unavoidable and containing stare impinged to the point of a transformation of the social figures with their orderly, knitted shadows, the well-groomed grass and the beds, worked out in this pattern.[10]

Being watched—which is, first of all, a literal fact, since the house is eventually to be the victim of ambush—here becomes also a figure for absolute powerlessness: the inhabitants of the house are possessed by this almost godlike and indifferent gaze, that of the agents of the history which will supercede them.

It is a point often made about those historical Big House novels set in the 1920s, initiated by *The Last September*, that in them the House becomes a literary property and symbol at the moment of its demise as a social fact, an emblem for the world that is lost. Certainly, such nostalgic phrases as 'in those days', or 'at that time', which Bowen employs and which are then taken up by others including Keane, Higgins, and J. G. Farrell, appear to give these historical fictions some of the usual appeal of retrospect. However, this is in fact very heavily qualified, as in *The Last September*, by a strong sense of the inherent instability and valuelessness of what has now vanished: a society of gossip, tennis parties, and tea, in which violence seems almost like another social engagement, to be met with the stiff upper lip of decorum. 'In those extraordinary days,' Molly Keane says in *Two Days in Aragon*, 'there was every chance of bloodshed after tea and tennis with strawberries and cream.'

In Elizabeth Bowen, however, who was the daughter and subsequently mistress of such a house herself, and its historian in the non-fictional *Bowen's Court* (1942), there is usually a tone of wistfulness or repining, whatever alternative tones are combined with it. Her other work is also often and sometimes surprisingly allusive to the image of the Big House. In her short story 'The Happy Autumn Fields', the time of the London Blitz is supernaturally crossed with that of a Big House in Victorian Ireland: an interpenetration in which the present is read as a tragic falling off, in a characteristic example of modernist nostalgia ('So much flowed through people; so little flows through us'). In her wartime novel *The Heat of the Day*, the Irish house Mount Morris represents the stability and permanence of a rooted ancestral order opposed to the unstable class position of the treacherous and pro-fascist Robert Kelway. As late as *A World of Love* (1955), the house Montefort becomes the vehicle for mysterious terminations and transitions, mergings of dead and living, past and present, and an education for Jane—the final *ingénue* in Bowen's work—in the knowledge of what it is to 'love'.

The Last September, set in 1920, combines a certain wistfulness with something much harder, more analytic and satiric, as the alternating lassitude and febrility of life at Danielstown impinge on Lois. The highly charged discontinuities of Bowen's style, which seems at the same moment both poised and reckless, saving itself from tremulousness by the strict exercise of will, may be regarded as a kind of Anglo-Irish stylistic hyphen. A duality and ambiguity of response is woven into the texture of her prose, which is the register of both a divided allegiance and the mixed feelings of retrospect.

The impermanence of the house in *The Last September* is implied in the titles of the book's three parts which name an 'Arrival', a 'Visit', and a 'Departure' (which is actually a death by murder) of the novel's characters. In 1920 the Big House is a temporary stay for the Anglo-Irish who drift through it on their way elsewhere; and the house itself is enjoying only a temporary stay of what the novel actually calls, as I have said, 'execution'. In this 'last September' Lois drifts into a kind of engagement with the English soldier Gerald; but this is his last September too, since he is killed by the IRA before their relationship comes to anything. The contrast between, and contiguity of, vaguely cultured leisure and sudden catastrophic violence, between the sometimes frozen politenesses of life inside the demesne walls and the danger lurking outside, is dramatized throughout the book, most vividly in a well-orchestrated scene in which Lois, in the company of the visitors to the house, Hugh and Marda, encounters an IRA man in hiding in an old mill. This ancient ruined mill—'strangled', as Hugh says, by 'English law', but nevertheless affecting him 'like a sense of the future; an unpleasant sensation of being tottered over'—seems, like the Majestic Hotel in *Troubles*, almost to represent Anglo-Ireland itself in its decline. The mill has entered 'the democracy of ghostliness', and is 'strangely set for a Watteau interlude', like the pastoral appurtenances of the Blue Drawing Room in Green's Kinalty Castle in *Loving*; and the cracks in its walls are explicitly likened to those in Poe's 'The Fall of the House of Usher', a text that may also lie behind Farrell's images of ruin in *Troubles*. In the violence of the encounter, in which Marda is shot and superficially wounded, these literary and artistic allusions make it seem almost as though a nuanced Jamesian novel of the finely sensitized mobility of human interrelationship, and of the *ingénue* woken to unsettling but maturing recognitions, has been suddenly and sickeningly appropriated by an influx of Conradian physical violence. The result for the characters is the immediate disintegration of the conventional but fragile Anglo-Irish *politesse*: 'transgressing the decencies' with 'awful unprivacy'.

For Elizabeth Bowen this intrusion of history into the world of 'privacy' is the deepest and most corrosive insult to the Big House 'aesthetic of living'. Contaminated in such a way, the House must either die or retain an almost posthumously depleted existence in the new, post-revolutionary Ireland. At the end of *The Last September* Danielstown does die, 'executed' by the IRA. Bowen's Court, which was the model for Danielstown, actually survived the burnings of the 1920s to become an ever-more taxing drain on Bowen's depleted finances, to be sold eventually in 1960 and immediately demolished. It is therefore tempting to read the end of *The Last September* as a register of desire as well as despair, the quick execution of the fictional house representing a Yeatsian preference for heroic endings over the fate of a tawdry and bathetic lingering-on. The final sentence of the novel reads: 'Above the steps the door stood open hospitably upon a furnace.' Even at its last, the House welcomes the flames with an eighteenth-century courtesy: host as well as victim to the end.

Molly Keane's historical fictions of the 1920s are written to some extent in the shadow of *The Last September*, but they also supply sophisticated variations of their own. Her current reputation is based primarily on the novels she published in the 1980s, after a long break in her writing life, particularly *Good Behaviour*, which carry the Big House novel into new areas of black farce and only just still-comic frightfulness. Although clearly revealing an author newly and peculiarly in her element, these novels are ultimately more conventional in their comic hyperbole than the more deeply unsettling modes of the earlier work. In both *Mad Puppetstown* and *Two Days in Aragon* the preoccupations of most of her novels with problematic or sadistic domestic relationships, with the maintenance of an insecure and anxious social veneer over awkward or unbearable private secrets, with the intense solitude of children and the loneliness and sexual yearning of young women, are brought to a new pitch of extremity by being plotted into and pitted against the terrifying political history of the time. In both books, domestic chaos and crisis are met by, and sucked remorselessly into, social disintegration and revolution; and the encounter between the two worlds, which is also the encounter between Anglo-Irish and Irish, inevitably issues in acts of violence, on which the plots turn. Keane's style, a hybrid like Bowen's, oscillates between a limpid plangency and a sudden acidic sharpness. Fluidly in motion, it is responsive to the interpenetration of the different worlds with which she deals.

There are elements of melodrama in these novels, when Keane deals with terrorist activity and its attempted suppression: in *Two Days in Aragon* she tries to pre-empt such criticism with a self-deprecating reference to the adventure stories of

R. M. Ballantyne. These elements should not, however, distract attention from what is of real moment and impact in the books: the convincing and intimately knowledgeable portrayal, from within, of the interconnections, indissoluble and tragic, between the different Irelands, which is managed with both delicacy and power. In *Two Days in Aragon* this is rendered primarily in the figure of Nan Foley, who is, like Shibby Pindy in *The Big House of Inver*, an illegitimate child of the Big House and now its jealous housekeeper. Her attempt to rescue her son from the IRA culminates in her own hideously ironic death when she is run down by a Black and Tan lorry. The theme is also focused through the sexual relationship between Nan's son, Foley O'Neill, and a daughter of the house, Grania Fox; and through the ultimate sexual collusion between the other daughter of the house, Sylvia, and the IRA man, Denny the Killer, who burns it down. The utterly unpredictable and class-crossing trajectories of sexual attraction make it seem almost as though at any moment political violence might be displaced by sexuality, or vice versa; and the book is a profound exploration of the pathology of a political culture in which such instabilities are endemic.

In *Mad Puppetstown*, this is also very much to the point: Patsy, the House's bootboy, has, for a brief time, a loyalty to the IRA 'that was almost as much lust of the flesh as it was an intoxication of the spirit'. The theme is, however, handled more interestingly, because more exceptionally, here since it is focused through Patsy's relationship in childhood with the children of the House, the witty and scathingly intelligent Easter and her cousins Basil and Evelyn. At the close of the War of Independence, Patsy, who has grown increasingly disillusioned with the methods of the IRA, returns to the house and runs it with its one remaining family member, the very old Aunt Dicksie, who has saved it from burning. When Easter inherits the house and returns to it with Basil after an unhappy period in England, the new relationships between classes and ages appear to act as the idealistic emblem for a different, more egalitarian mode of organization of the Big House, one more consistent with the social principles and aims of the Irish Free State.

There is an astonishing moment at the very end of the novel when Easter visits the local village to view 'the smallest house in Ireland', little more than a lean-to, which is shared by an adulterous, outlawed couple and their 'love-child'. In contrast to her feelings about the houses she has known in England, where she has failed to find true attachment or affection (Luddington Court, outside Oxford, plays its exquisite but shallow refinement over a social, cultural, and spiritual void), her emotion at the sight of the outlaw father accompanying his dancing child on the flute outside their 'small house' is invested with a utopian feeling for the affections attaching to a home which might be shared by Anglo-Irish gentry and Catholic Irish peasant. The moment is managed without sentimentality, but it may nevertheless seem an idealistic mystification of actual economic and social difference; although Easter's unusual forename, having associations with both the Easter Rising of 1916 and the Christian Resurrection, may well signal the radical nature of the gesture being made here. As a frail and tentative emblem of possible complementarity and mutual aspiration, woven through with courtesy, apology, and kindness, it has an empathy deriving from the now shared experience of loss and dispossession. It powerfully both foreshadows and answers the image of the 'lovers and the dancers . . . beaten into the clay' in 'The Curse of Cromwell', another poem by Yeats referential to the Big House, published in his *New Poems* (1938). It is testimony to the social and imaginative density and complexity of Molly Keane's deceptively unassuming work that it can articulate such things, with tact.

3. *Reconstructions, Simulacra*

The durability of the fictional representation of the Big House in the 1920s, and its usefulness as the means of new effects and significances, is apparent in two novels published in the early 1970s, J. G. Farrell's *Troubles* and John Banville's *Birchwood*. Brendan Archer in *Troubles* has returned to England after the First World War vaguely shell-shocked and, in a fit of distraction, appears to have entered into an 'understanding' with Angela Spencer, the daughter of an Anglo-Irish household; but this understanding turns out in fact to be his initiation into an elaborate series of tragicomic misunderstandings. The novel traces his progress, or regress, in the period of the War of Independence, as he becomes deeply entangled with this household, that of the dilapidated Majestic Hotel in Kilnalough, Co. Wexford, run by Angela's father Edward; and as, after Angela's mysterious death, he enters into an endlessly frustrating and deferred relationship with the local, Catholic *femme fatale* and *belle dame sans merci*, Sarah Devlin. This relationship brings him into immediate contact with a world usually left in the margins of the Big House novel, that of the Catholic Irish bourgeoisie who will inherit the country after the foundation of the Irish Free State in 1922.

At first completely uncomprehending of, and bored by, Irish politics, Brendan Archer—usually referred to more anonymously as 'the Major'—is ultimately forced to live them in the most intimate and dangerous ways. In the first quarter of 1919, the novel tells us, there are thirty-six murders, and the Major witnesses one on a visit to Dublin. He subsequently has to tidy up the mess after the increasingly crazed Edward murders an assumed member of the IRA; and the novel culminates in his own last-minute rescue from a hideous death, after he has been buried up to the head on the strand to await the incoming tide. The plot of *Troubles* might be defined as the Major's gradual redefinition for himself of the complicated word 'Irish', in tandem with a growing scepticism, as he witnesses the brutality of the Black and Tans, about what he at first unquestioningly calls the 'moral authority' of the British in Ireland ('The cure may be as bad as the disease', he says grimly). This British 'Major' is, then, brought to a crisis of readjusted political and moral perspective by his time in the 'Majestic', one of the last retreats of Empire, with its statue of Queen Victoria on the front lawn and its rotting 'Imperial Bar'.

The Major is Farrell's reconstruction of a type prominent in the fictions of modernism after the First World War: the displaced or superfluous man who suffers the guilt of the survivor. A returnee from the war, part of whose mind is permanently lodged there among the dead, without significant family roots or ties in England, and lacking the ability to construct new emotional or sexual ties for himself, the Major's superfluity is in profound harmony with that of the Anglo-Irish he encounters in Kilnalough; and the novel moves through a series of weary, if also comic, ironies, incongruities, and disparities, in an atmosphere of what Elizabeth Bowen, in a highly commendatory review, brilliantly called 'unavailingness'.[11] Farrell succeeds in making the Major both a sympathetic representative of his type and, at the same time, an irritatingly passive and withdrawn example of the type too, so that when he is maltreated by Sarah, at least some of the reader's sympathies are with her. This does not, however, mitigate the pain of the anti-climax of their relationship, when the Major overcomes the deepest isolation of his reserve only to be met with a cavalierly self-interested indifference.

The poignancy of the Major's unhappy personal story, which culminates in his abandonment and abjection, is incorporated in the larger politics of Ireland between 1919 and 1921. In that story the Majestic Hotel becomes a metonym for the fate of Anglo-Ireland: its sign has lost its letter 'C'; its statue of Victoria is an incitement to IRA attack; and its proprietor Edward Spencer disintegrates into megalomania and homicide (his name recalls that of the Elizabethan poet and colonist Edmund Spenser, whose *View of the Present State of Ireland* (1598) ambivalently recommended genocide). In one of the book's most striking (if also slightly mechanical) narrative devices, these interpenetrating stories are interrupted every so often by contemporary press reports of global political crisis and revolution in the 1920s— notably in Capone's Chicago, Lenin's Russia, and Gandhi's India. These serve to make the implications of the novel's title ramify so that the 'troubles' of the personal life are located within a displacing political and historical context: not at the centre, but very much at the edge of a network of interrelating violent struggles for power. Caught in such a web of interconnectedness, the Major's decent and generous-hearted liberalism, with its guilts, shames, and helplessness, seems itself superfluous. The view of history in *Troubles* is one in which the effectiveness of personal action is severely circumscribed by larger forces of dominance and manipulation. The form of the novel therefore both expresses and places in perspective the reach of a tolerant liberal humanism in a revolutionary period. The best kind of historical fiction, it manages what Charles Palliser has characterized as 'an almost Tolstoyan objectivity' by evoking a past 'whose political, economic and ideological contradictions are understood without being patronized'.[12]

In *Birchwood*, John Banville uses many of the themes and motifs of Big House fiction as the vehicle for an elaborately intertextual pastiche. A sort of *fantasia* on themes from the Big House, a long way from the modes of realism and naturalism which sustain most examples of the genre, the novel is primarily a self-reflexive and writerly fiction. In addition to generalized allusions to numerous Irish Big House novels, reference is also made to a range of other texts, notably Dickens (Banville has the audacity to borrow the audacious death by spontaneous combustion from *Bleak House*), Proust, Beckett, Joyce, Wittgenstein, Descartes, and, pre-eminently, Nabokov. The novel's style of fastidiously precise, even pedantic, luxuriance—almost oxymoronically both elegant and exorbitant—calls great attention to itself; and the writer eventually appears more or less explicitly as a kind of Prospero, and is also figured anagramatically in the hero's temporary pseudonym, 'Johann Livelb' ('John Banville').

These imaginative tricks and treats are played along with a Big House narrative in which motifs of twinning and quest are salient. The novel's hero, Gabriel Godkin, is the victim of his Aunt Martha's deception. To effect his disinheritance in favour of her own son, Michael, she persuades Gabriel to undertake an extended search for his twin sister, Rose. Towards the end of his quest-journey, in the revelation of a hitherto secret plot, Gabriel realizes that he has been duped, that he has no twin sister, and that Michael is in fact his half-brother, incestuously conceived by his father and Aunt Martha. In a lengthy and violent climax apparently set during the Civil War of 1922 (although the novel is never temporally specific), Gabriel disposes of Michael and finally comes into his inheritance. In the spring season of the book's closing pages he decides to 'live a life different from any the house has ever known'; but in an ambiguous move utterly characteristic of this duplicitous novel, what he actually does is to write or 'invent' the past in the narrative we have just read. *Birchwood* ends with this irresolute Janus facing both past and future, solipsistically static before the 'white landscape' of the unwritten page.

This plot gives Banville scope to range through a theatrical stock or museum of Big House effects, parading his own ingenuity as the maker of a new kind of patchwork fiction out of the bits and pieces of apparently almost unusably over-familiar motifs. Such Nabokovian cunning, however, in which the house is above all a literary cipher or postmodern simulacrum, 'all emptiness and echo', waiting to be filled with quotation and citation, may also be read as a more Joycean cunning too: it acts as an aesthetic disguise for political insinuation. When Gabriel leaves the house of Birchwood in order to undertake his quest, he is leaving the walled, if ruined, demesne of Anglo-Irish history for the barbaric violence of peasant Irish history. Beyond the demesne is the world of Prospero's Magic Circus which is, on one level, a knowing amalgam of literary fragments (Herman Hesse, Alain-Fournier, Dickens's *Hard Times*); but is, on another, the opportunity for a hallucinatory transmission of some of the most intractable facts of Irish history, from the Cromwellian atrocities of the seventeenth century, through the Famines of 1845 and afterwards, to the terrorism of the 'Molly Maguires' and the Black and Tans in the War of Independence. Prospero's Circus, running the horrors of Irish history through its hoops and highwire acts, is the metonymic location in which Gabriel—son of the Big House newly transformed into 'Livelb', the disguised name of his creator—is forced into confrontation with everything hitherto entirely alien to him.

It is in this context that the novel's motifs of twinning and *doppelgänger*, and an associated imagery of mirror and echo, should also be read. The 'civilization' of the house Birchwood is made permeable to the chaotically 'barbaric' circus of the world outside, the world of repression and oppression which nevertheless sustains it economically. Similarly, Gabriel is forced to recognize his incestuous twinning with Michael: inside the House of Anglo-Irish civility the good and bad angels, both of them intelligent and artful, war for dominance. The epigraph to *Birchwood* is Catullus' 'Odi et amo' ('I hate and I love; ask how? I cannot tell you | Only I feel it, and I am torn in two'); and the novel finds, in its own twinning of House and hinterland, a series of emblems for oppositional and deeply held views of 'Ireland'.

In its marriage of a densely allusive literary prose with some of the most appalling facts of Irish historical suffering, *Birchwood* also offers testimony to writerly scruple. By refusing the antici-pated pathos of engagement—by, as it were, placing such pathos before a distorting mirror, or sounding it in a ridiculously rever-berant echo-chamber—it offers for consideration one model of the writer's obligation towards received national, political, and cultural images. Interrogating tropes and stereotypes, it also dramatizes, like *Troubles*, the ways in which the historical novel might be scrupulously referential to the present moment of its composition as well as to the past moment of its representation: since *Troubles* and *Birchwood*, both published in the early 1970s, contain within their historical fictions the knowledge of the return of these barely repressed historical distresses in the political history of Northern Ireland after 1968.

4. Peacock's Feathers

This being so, it is unsurprising that a preoccupation with the Big House, as social reality and literary tradition, surfaces again in contemporary Irish poetry, including some work from the North. In 'A Visit to Castletown House', Michael Hartnett attends a concert in one of the most splendid Georgian houses in Ireland, but his enjoyment of Paul Tortelier is deeply interrupted by his nationalist sense of the house's violently repressive history:

> I stepped into the gentler evening air
> and saw black figures dancing on the lawn,
> Eviction, Droit de Seigneur, Broken Bones:
> and heard the crack of ligaments being torn
> and smelled the clinging blood upon the stones.

Derek Mahon's 'A Disused Shed in Co. Wexford' is dedicated to J. G. Farrell and may be thought to derive its imagery of fungoid growth, of the patient mushrooms that 'have been waiting for us in a foetor | Of vegetable sweat since civil war days', from *Troubles*; and it develops that imagery into a profound and inclusive meditation on historical suffering, desolation, and abandonment. Thomas Kinsella's 'Tao and Unfitness, at Inistiogue on the River Nore' meditates on the un-Irish Irish village near Kilkenny—'perfectly lovely, | like a typical English village'—in which the burned-out house of Woodstock becomes for this poet 'a flitting-place | for ragged feeling, old angers and rumours' of Black and Tan days. Paul Muldoon's 'The Big House' and poems by Tom Paulin, including 'At Maas' and 'Mount Stewart', also play original variations on the theme; but one of the most notable poetic explorations of it is Seamus Heaney's 'A Peacock's Feather', published in his volume *The Haw Lantern* in 1987, but dated 1972.

The date of composition is significant, since it is the date of publication of Heaney's volume *Wintering Out*, the first book of his to respond to the situation in Northern Ireland after 1968. The poem is an occasional piece in octosyllabic couplets, the form used in 'Upon Appleton House' and 'The Garden' by Andrew Marvell, those seventeenth-century poems celebrating English country houses. It is written to commemorate the christening of an 'English niece', born into what appears to be a house of some splendour in Gloucestershire. Heaney represents himself as self-consciously at work on the poem in the house itself and, writing as an Irishman from outside the estate walls, having to 'level' his 'cart-track voice to garden tones'. The situation presents him with a wry but embarrassed or, as it were, extramural analogy: 'I might as well be in Coole Park.' The poem therefore contains both the generosity of doing the decent thing by family obligation and also the guilt of behaving so unlike himself, and the people he comes from, as to strike the Yeatsian pose. This mixed feeling issues in a final stanza in which a nationalist resentment at centuries of oppression inevitably gets in the way of any ease of celebration or petition for the christening of this child of an English house. The metaphor here, which mixes the shed blood of history with the maternal milk, seems an obdurate insistence, almost despite the poem's own good-will, on the deep and permanent estrangements of those inside and outside the walls. It is an estrangement made all the more poetically powerful by Heaney's importation from Yeats's sequence 'Meditations in Time of Civil War' of the symbolic peacock which 'strays' on 'some rich man's flowering lawns' in one poem and 'screams' at the end of another:

> So before I leave your ordered home,
> Let us pray. May tilth and loam,
> Darkened with Celts' and Saxons' blood,
> Breastfeed your love of house and wood—
> Where I drop this for you, as I pass,
> Like the peacock's feather on the grass.

3

Lyrical Fields and Featherbeds: Representations of the Rural and the Provincial

The world looks on
And talks of the peasant:
The peasant has no worries;
In his little lyrical fields
He ploughs and sows . . .
Without the peasant base civilisation must die,
Unless the clay is in the mouth the singer's singing is useless.

(Patrick Kavanagh, *The Great Hunger*)

. . . the soft smother of the provincial featherbed.

(Sean O'Faolain, *Vive Moi!*)

1. Image, Counter-Image

One of the main aims of the Irish Literary Revival had been to establish a literature in English which was nevertheless distinctively Irish; and one of the primary ways in which this aim had been advanced, notably in Yeats's poetry, was by providing an image of Irish rural life—particularly of life in the West—which would act as a model for various types of moral and artistic behaviour. The rural image would represent a tested, endured solitude and the generous supportiveness of community; the patient effort of labour and the nobility of suffering; the ideal of dedication and the reward of courage. Yeats's imagery of the West and his portrayal of its heroized figures—such as the Connemara hero of the poem 'The Fisherman', a 'wise and simple man' invented in contradistinction to the 'insolent', opportunistic urban society Yeats presents himself as enduring—

constituted an inescapably powerful and influential mode of representing rural Ireland and a richly ceremonious national idea.

The authority of the image was persuasively reinforced by the clutch of autobiographical accounts of life on the remote Blasket Islands, off the coast of Kerry, which appeared in the late 1920s and 1930s: Tomás O Criomhthain's *An tOileánach* (*The Islandman*) (1929), Maurice O'Sullivan's *Fiche Blian ag Fás* (*Twenty Years A-Growing*) (1933), and Peig Sayers's *Peig* (1936). E. M. Forster wrote an introduction to *Twenty Years A-Growing* which describes it as 'an account of neolithic civilization from the inside', one in which the neolithic 'has itself become vocal, and addressed modernity'.[1] This 'address' is a crucial feature of Forster's high regard: he is impressed by the way O'Sullivan is at one and the same time 'neolithic' and cultured in a modern manner (he likes the movies, Forster tells us). This dimension of O'Sullivan's experience, however, and of the work itself, tended to become occluded in the sentimental reception given to these books. In fact, they tell the tale not of an attainable perennial ideal but of a civilization on its last legs. It is their reception, and that of other books in Irish not altogether unlike them, but much less valuable than them, rather than the books themselves that Flann O'Brien scathingly satirizes in his parody of the genre, *An Béal Bocht* (*The Poor Mouth*) (1941), with its narrative of complaint, petition, servility, opportunism, and endless rain.

If the idea of the rural that figures in Yeats is one model of Irishness inherited by the writers who succeeded him, another is that to be found in the rhetoric of the founders of the Irish Free State. To a large degree, post-revolutionary Irish society was obscurantist, inward-turning, economically and culturally protectionist in some of the classic post-colonial ways; and it was also a society whose rural patterns and attitudes maintained some continuity with those of the latter half of the nineteenth century.[2] As part of its ideology, therefore, it promoted the notion of an 'Irish Ireland' associated with the state-imposed revival of the language (through its obligatory use in the education system), with the moral teaching of the Catholic Church (which was given a 'special position' in the Constitution of 1937), and with the idealization of rural life as a bastion against the modernizing forces of urban, Anglo-American, and European civilization, a bastion well-defended by the tenets of the Censorship of Publications Act of 1929, which provided for the banning of a large number of the works of classic and modern literature. This ideology was given notorious expression in a radio broadcast made by Eamon de Valera on St Patrick's Day, 1943, when he celebrated the ideal which had informed the nationalist politics of the Irish state throughout the 1930s. The passage has been quoted so often in commentary on post-1920s Ireland as to make its further citation virtually a cliché, but it does make the point as nothing else can:

That Ireland which we dreamed of would be the home of a people who valued material wealth only as a basis of right living, of a people who were satisfied with frugal comfort and devoted their leisure to the things of the spirit; a land whose countryside would be bright with cosy homesteads, whose fields and villages would be joyous with sounds of industry, the romping of sturdy children, the contests of athletic youths, the laughter of comely maidens; whose firesides would be the forums of the wisdom of serene old age.[3]

It is difficult to understand now how the comic-book Homeric pastoral of that could ever have carried the authority that it did, although English readers may well recognize a not entirely dissimilar kind of appeal at work in such books as Laurie Lee's *Cider with Rosie* (1959). It was a nationalist self-image developed out of the psycho- and socio-pathology of post-colonial experience, and developed to some extent as a sentimentalizing of certain actual persistences, of the kind catalogued in such writings as E. Estyn Evans's *Irish Heritage* (1943) and *Irish Folk Ways* (1957) and also much later in some of Seamus Heaney's prose, notably his essay 'The Sense of Place' (1977), in which he remembers his rural childhood in Co. Derry in the 1940s and 1950s. The image had become hopelessly outmoded with the economic reforms of Seán Lemass and T. K. Whitaker in the late 1950s and early 1960s, and was given its final kiss of death with

Ireland's entry into the EEC in 1972, when the economic benefits of the Common Agricultural Policy effectively brought to an end many of the established social relations and forms of rural life. The way the image was subsequently marketed as part of a 'heritage' industry is effectively satirized in Brian Friel's play *The Communication Cord* (1982), in which an old cottage, newly converted, becomes the setting for a farce concerning contemporary Irish venality, hypocrisy, and opportunism. As long as it lasted, however, the idealized image was very successfully advanced both at home and abroad (particularly in America), and in the face of an Irish reality in many respects altogether different from its smug self-approbation: one not of 'frugality' but of poverty; not of domesticity but of emigration; not of 'industry' but of unemployment; not of families of happy children but of a celibacy necessitated by economic circumstance; not of 'serenity' but of anxiety.

Both Yeats's and de Valera's stereotypes were very influential, however, on some of the work produced in the period after Yeats. In such typical poems as Padraic Colum's 'Plougher' and F. R. Higgins's 'Father and Son', the mythologizing of the rural labourer persists in what seems, after the self-assurance and aplomb of Yeats's figuration, an already tired and vitiated mode. Patrick Kavanagh's work also begins in quasi-Yeatsian myth-making: his own 'Ploughman', published in 1930, finds 'a star-lovely art | In a dark sod', and there is a delighted aboriginal uplift in his address 'To the Man after the Harrow' ('For you are driving your horses through | The mist where Genesis begins') that almost out-Yeatses Yeats in its positing of archetypal pattern and mythological precedent. It is, nevertheless, Kavanagh who decisively breaks with the Yeatsian model; and, although his poetry may well seem to some only approximately and intermittently successful, producing its genuine achievements from a sometimes apparently bedraggled flurry of the flimsy and the throw-away, these successes have been enormously influential.

Kavanagh was a self-taught small farmer in Inniskeen, Co. Monaghan, until, when over the age of 30, he left for Dublin. *The Great Hunger* (1942) is a long poem dealing with the expe-

rience of a Co. Monaghan farmer, Patrick Maguire. Its chronologically non-sequential vignettes trace him from young manhood to old age. Subjected to mother, Church, and land, he leads
a life of celibacy interrupted only by masturbation and sexual
fantasizing, until the impotence of age, when he has become
petrified into 'respectability and righteousness', and until an
imagined afterlife in which 'He will hardly remember what has
happened to him'. The poem's fourteen parts construct a pano-
ramic vista of his emotionally depleted circumstances—'the grey
and grief and unlove'—and sustain a painfully ironic correlation
between a working life devoted to the fertility of the land and a
sexual life atrophied at its very source: he is praised by his
mother as 'the man who made a field his bride'—which may, of
course, be interpreted otherwise than the way she presumably
intends. Some of the poem's finest evocations are of an isolated
evening world of unfulfilled desire, of crepuscular longings in
which Maguire's knowledge of attenuated possibility meets his
sense, at the very edge of consciousness, of another kind of life
when 'He would be a new man walking through unbroken
meadows | Of dawn in the year of One'. This visionary
utopianism is consonant with both Kavanagh's intimate knowledge of Irish emigrant desire, and also with his own sense of
poetic distinctiveness as it is recorded in his autobiographical
novel *Tarry Flynn* (1948):

Was there not a second Tarry of whom nobody in Drumnay was aware,
not even his mother, who looked on at the mortal Tarry, watching,
laughing, criticizing and recording? He saw himself sitting there in the
corner with his elbows on the table while his mother and sisters talked.
Though he was silent his was the only opinion that would matter in the
long run.[4]

The arrogant self-assurance of this is characteristic of
Kavanagh's work, although it is combined elsewhere with many
kinds of vulnerability. It is undoubtedly the quality which
prompted the revolutionary energy of *The Great Hunger*, which
took on and deconstructed the sentimentalities and idealizations
of Irish literary tradition and ideological self-promotion.

The poem's thirteenth section engages these images at an explicit, satirical level, castigating those who imagine the peasant 'in his little lyrical fields' able to 'talk to God as Moses and Isaiah talked': *The Great Hunger*, a poem devoted to the traducing of stereotype, knows that the peasant is actually 'half a vegetable'. This polemic is prosecuted, in a poem which has its theatrical dimension, through the narratorial style, which is manipulatively directive of the reader, with constant direct questions and commands, busily organizing attitude and response.[5] This has led some critics to argue that there is an element of 'over-determination' in the work;[6] but it can equally well be suggested that what Kavanagh very successfully manages is a style which oscillates between empathy and judgement. The empathy recognizes and exposes individual suffering, while the rhetoric of satire and invective castigates social disease. This bifocal vision, recorded in a mixture of realistic and rhetorically heightened modes, is exactly what the poem's title intends. Usually the phrase by which the historical catastrophe of the Irish Famine of the mid-nineteenth century is known, it refers in this poem to the metaphorical 'hunger' of a people for emotional, intellectual, and sexual sustenance. As such, it may well be thought to make an almost melodramatic claim on our attention; but in fact, as Terence Brown has shown, it was precisely the Famine itself, and its aftermath in Irish society and consciousness, which promoted the peculiar economic and social arrangements—particularly the requirement of adult celibacy—which control Maguire's existence.[7] Undoubtedly too the title deflates the pieties of nationalism by presenting a Free State 'famine' for which England cannot be blamed. The title, therefore, binds together contemporary individual experience and the patterns of continuing Irish social and economic history; and the achievement of *The Great Hunger* is to have articulated a representative socially and culturally constructed psyche in its complex inwardness, and to have offered this as a radical counter-image to the offensively appropriative stereotype.

Kavanagh's rural imagery, however, is not all as negative as this, even in *The Great Hunger* itself, where an indictment of the Catholic Church's complicity in repression is balanced by a visionary nature mysticism congruent with Catholic orthodoxy. The celebratory note which this strikes in the poem, cutting across its despondency, is echoed elsewhere in Kavanagh's work too, where, in poems such as 'Iniskeen Road, July Evening', 'Spraying the Potatoes', 'Kerr's Ass', and 'A Christmas Childhood', the actualities of Irish rural life are made fully available, for the first time, to poetry in the English language (although some of the work of Joseph Cambell and, arguably, Padraic Colum may be thought to precede Kavanagh in something of the same spirit). Kavanagh developed an affirmative trust in the way his own rural place was a fit subject for poetry into his influential theory of the distinction between the 'parochial' and the 'provincial'. In his critical work the former term is purged of its usual derogatory connotations to become the approved alternative to the phoney kinds of 'Irishness' which inhere in the 'provincial' mentality:

Parochialism and provincialism are opposites. The provincial has no mind of his own: he does not trust what his eyes see until he has heard what the metropolis—towards which his eyes are turned—has to say ... The parochial mentality, on the other hand, is never in any doubt about the social and artistic validity of his parish. All great civilizations are based on the parish—Greek, Israelite, English.[8]

The poem 'Epic' gives the critique imaginative expression with a humour and dignity which avoid self-importance even in the act of defining what it is to have 'lived in important places' and discovering significance in a local (or 'parochial') row rather than in the world war about to begin in the 1938 of its recalled historical moment:

> That was the year of the Munich bother. Which
> Was more important? I inclined
> To lose my faith in Ballyrush and Gortin
> Till Homer's ghost came whispering to my mind.
> He said: I made the *Iliad* from such
> A local row. Gods make their own importance.

Kavanagh's work, even if it does, as I have claimed, include a strong subconsciousness or 'political unconscious' (as Fredric Jameson has defined the phrase)[9] of what it is to have been formed by historical events such as the Famine, is entirely lacking in any more explicit historical sense. Like Beckett, Kavanagh may have designedly rejected the Yeatsian use of the past as a means of measuring the present. He is never tempted into historical or mythological reference, and is never, therefore, seduced by a Yeatsian rhetoric. Padraic Fallon, who grew up in Athenry, Co. Galway, was a member of the same poetic generation as Kavanagh and was in fact deeply learned in history and myth. Consequently, he had more of a struggle with the Yeatsian heritage. Still seriously underrated, partly because of the peculiar publishing history in which his first book appeared only in 1974, a few months before his death—previously he had published only in magazines and anthologies—Fallon offers a vibrant alternative to the realism of Kavanagh and, eventually in his career, a mythologically renewed version of the West which is referential to, but also combative with the ghost of Yeatsian grandeur.

As he puts it in 'For Paddy Mac', an elegy for the poet Patrick MacDonagh, there were in his West 'No poets I know of; or they mouthed each other's words; | Such low powered gods | They died, as they were born, in byres'; and consequently he tackles the Yeatsian inheritance directly in poems such as 'Yeats at Athenry, Perhaps' and 'Stop on the Road to Ballylee'. His own West, 'this | Waterhaunted ledge of the Atlantic', is perceived in its inherited cultural, social, and religious forms and political history, particularly the history of the eighteenth century, with its penal repressions, hedge schools, and outlaw poets such as Raftery. This historical density is deepened further with a personal synthesis of classical, Eastern, and Native American mythologies and with a range of modern and modernist European and American poetic influences (notably Ezra Pound). Although the result is sometimes headily opaque, the effect can also be to purify the image of the West of its standard Yeatsian colorations. Fallon's best work offers a native vision of an Irish rural life not glamorized, appropriated, or exploited, but turned into an intense kind of interior self-communing. For all its occasional esotericism, this appears uncondescendingly continuous with the kinds of conversation Fallon might have had with the rural figures named and evoked in some of his poems. Although the work sometimes seems strained in its large ambition, and although, deriving from great creative isolation, it can have a debilitating literariness, its major successes, such as 'Gurteen', 'A Hedge Schoolmaster', and 'The Small Town of John Coan' feed on the transformative energies supplied by his unlikely juxtapositions and collocations. When 'The Small Town of John Coan' presents an image of the poet as 'the leafy boy | Scored in the dapple, his small footprints | In the midst of great improbable events', Fallon intends, I think, both the actual events of modern Irish and European history and also those imaginative events that take place in the intricately composite mythological synthesis of his own poems. His work itself stands uniquely 'in the midst' of these perhaps improbable but certainly renovating cross-currents.

2. *Locations and Dislocations*

In decisively breaking with Yeatsian modes of Romantic mythologizing, then, rural Irish poets of the mid-century also made it clear how inseparable from matters of Irish history and ideology representations of rural Ireland are: whether because the Famine is inscribed so deeply into the Irish landscape and psyche—however inscrutably in individual cases—or because of the deValeran valorization of an impossible ideal, or because, in a colonial and post-colonial country, matters of the land's ownership are inevitably of more constantly perturbing moment than they are in less historically fraught and fractured political communities. In many other post-Yeatsian poets of Irish rural life, particularly those from the North, these recognitions are also made, even in the act of establishing particular Irish topographies with great imaginative definition and richness.

John Hewitt's Glens of Antrim, for instance, offer an urban poet, throughout a lengthy career, opportunities of assuagement in times of political stress, whether the Second World War or the Northern Irish Troubles. They provide a location in which the poet is intimately attuned to natural process and season, where his 'hand twitches with the leaping verse | as hazel twig will wrench the straining wrists' ('The Glens'). However, he is also acutely aware, in this landscape of solace, of his own outsider status, not only because he is urban but because he is Protestant where the farmers of the Glens are predominantly Catholic. The Glens therefore become the focus of anxiety in the same moment in which they are palliative; and they act, in the fullness of Hewitt's work, as a place of complex, even paradoxical allegiance: the location of the colonist's guilt, which is accompanied by the desire to make reparation, but also the place of an insistent territorial claim.

John Montague's Tyrone is partly, in poems such as 'The Water Carrier', in which he discovers a 'living source' in 'fictive water', the location of personal growth and epiphany, in modes inherited from a Wordsworthian tradition; but the rural is also figured in the way the title of his first volume, published in 1961, *Poisoned Lands*, implies. In such poems as 'Like Dolmens Round my Childhood, the Old People', the inhabitants of his rural origins are evoked in what Montague reads as some of the crabbed repressions of their psychological and cultural forms, including those of sectarianism. The poem consequently derides the Yeatsian conception of 'ancient Ireland': the reality is the almost splutteringly irritated alliteration of a 'Fomorian fierceness of family and local feud'. His well-known later poem, 'The Wild Dog Rose', in which the poet is told, and repeats, 'a story so terrible | that I try to push it away, | my bones melting'—the story of a drunken rape—moves the poetic expression of rural depredation a stage beyond Kavanagh's depictions in *The Great Hunger*.

At the end of 'Like Dolmens' the poet, standing in an ancient Irish stone circle, imagines the figures of his childhood passing into 'that dark permanence of ancient forms'. This is partly a trope for the way the poem itself acts as the imaginative salve for, and redress of the wounds of upbringing and formative consciousness, but it is also an indication of one of the fundamental perceptive modes of Montague's work, in which, as it develops, the idea of the Irish countryside takes on a very different connotation. In many of his poems the rural landscape is scrutinized for 'ancient forms' in the sense of the radiant traces of history and prehistory. Underwritten by a nationalist politics, and informed by an intimacy with the work of the Anglo-Welsh poetic mythographer David Jones, Montague's work becomes thereby, in sequences like 'A Slow Dance' (1975), the turning of the Irish rural world into a myth of continuity, tradition, and succession in which, for all the violence of the history recalled, the mind finds a fit for itself in a landscape intellectualized into revelation.

Seamus Heaney has written critical essays on both Kavanagh and Fallon and is a knowledgeable inheritor of their ways of reading Irish rural experience, even while also acutely receptive to the forms in which a range of English and American poets from Wordsworth, through Robert Frost, to Ted Hughes have interpreted the rural theme. Heaney's re-creation of his Co. Derry background is, from the beginning, then, very prominently generated out of his response to other literature as well as to personal experience and memory, and he began as a poet, he has said, when his roots were crossed with his reading.[10] It is a very knowing and self-knowing poet who opens his first collection, as Heaney opens *Death of a Naturalist* (1966), with a poem rhyming the pen with the spade, and therefore promoting a conception of the poem's continuity with the world of rural work and with the quotidian life of his own rural family. Throughout his career Heaney has consistently returned to the imagery of his origins for metaphors and figures in which a developing intellectual, cultural, and political life has articulated and inspected itself. Indeed, one of the most remarkable aspects of his work is that it has shown such a capacity to generate ramifyingly inclusive meanings and implications from a relatively narrow range of rural imagery.

That the poetry is always more than mere description and evocation is apparent when, in one of his finest early poems, 'At a Potato Digging', the mundane activity of digging for potatoes recalls to Heaney's imagination the sufferings of the rural Irish during the 1845 Famine, when the potato crop failed. Heaney looks at this landscape with an eye educated by the facts of Irish history. As in Montague, the land is densely recessive, a script which knowledge can teach the poet to read. This is one of the ways in which, as Heaney puts it in the sequence 'Singing School' in *North* (1975), quoting Wallace Stevens, 'Description is revelation'. Hence he evokes potato drills, bogland, farmyards, wells, springs, riverbanks, peninsulas with an impassioned but level, clear-eyed attentiveness to texture and contour; and in the actuality of such description rural Derry and, later in the work, Wicklow also become well-founded metaphors for a Wordsworthian study of the 'growth of a poet's mind'. Further, for all that he admires Kavanagh's depictions of rural depredation in *The Great Hunger*, Heaney is at least equally drawn to the older poet's more affectionate recallings of his originary Monaghan, finding in them 'revelation and confirmation';[11] and his own presentation, while it shares something of Kavanagh's ambivalence—the volume *Station Island* (1984) gives notable expression to moods of disenchantment and rejection—is predominantly a deeply affectionate and genial one, discovering in rural origin the sustenance of constant imaginative renewal.

It is possible that this affection is partly the product of Heaney's having been born a Northern Catholic. Subject neither to the repressions nor to the ideological distortions of the rural in the history of the Free State and the Republic, the Catholic North may have been afforded (along with the manifest injustices perpetrated on it in the course of its divided history) the paradoxical imaginative luxury of a relatively unsullied, even to some degree politically subversive sense of the rural. Without explicitly spelling out the political implications, Heaney registers an awareness of something like this when, in his essay 'The Sense of Place', he records the fact that he feels privileged to have experienced a way of life now virtually vanished from the western world and increasingly from Ireland itself. He writes of this world—with its calendar customs, its folk rhythms, seasonal cycles and instinct for the numinous—in ways that define a

Catholic childhood in the North, and identify in it a source of fundamental value. In one of his finest poems, 'The Harvest Bow' in *Field Work* (1979), he gives ample testimony to what is for him the permanent imaginative value of the Irish rural. The poem binds into its own intricate form a memory of his father's binding of the harvest bow itself, in what was a time-hallowed ritual at the end of the harvest period. The father's rural inarticulacy—in which he is continuous with Kavanagh's Maguire—is now, in the articulacy of the poem, given expression by the extremely articulate poet-son; and 'The Harvest Bow' culminates with the poet 'gleaning the unsaid off the palpable': drawing, in that rural metaphor (to 'glean' is literally to gather the newly reaped corn), the lesson of a filial fidelity which is at once successfully independent, self-assured and gratefully in-debted. It is also one of the truest lessons to be learnt about the relationship between art (making poems as well as making har-vest bows) and the quality of human life:

> *The end of art is peace*
> Could be the motto of this frail device
> That I have pinned up on our deal dresser—
> Like a drawn snare
> Slipped lately by the spirit of the corn
> Yet burnished by its passage, and still warm.

If Heaney's Derry is the best-known instance of rural repre-sentation in post-Yeatsian Irish poetry, there are also many others, all defining particular areas of the country as locations of the imagination too. Louis MacNeice's West, in poems such as 'The Strand' and 'Western Landscape', is the scene of grateful identification for a poet in many other ways rootlessly cosmo-politan, and also the location, in 'Neutrality', for a bitter repu-diation of Ireland's policy during the Second World War. Richard Murphy's Galway, in volumes such as *Sailing to an Island* (1963) and *High Island* (1974), is an elemental world of 'land-work and sea-fear' in which definitions of human identity are forged out of encounters with extreme natural forces, par-ticularly those of the sea itself. Derek Mahon's North Antrim and Derry coastlines are lonely, haunted topographies mutely offering testimony to various kinds of human desolation and abandonment. Michael Longley's botanically efflorescent Mayo is a landscape where natural flowerings and fadings frequently act as consolation or palliative for urban and psychological distress, but also figure as reminders of human mortality, taking their place in his work's preoccupation with metamorphosis and mutability. The North Antrim coastline in the work of Medbh McGuckian is an interiorized, feminized, and figuratively transformed, but still recognizable, marine topography in which states of being and consciousness are given fictive local correlatives. In the work of Nuala Ní Dhomnaill the rural landscapes of the South West, already much written into Irish literature, are newly rewritten, or written over, by a feminist mythologizing, energetically transformed by her 'exultant singing spirit', her 'ululations of grief', as they are named in the poem 'Destiny' in *The Astrakhan Cloak* (1992).

Much modern Irish poetry is, therefore, before it is anything else, a cartography of passionate natural piety. Nevertheless, images drawn from the Irish countryside in these poets all waver, as I have suggested, between actual location and some more imaginative metaphorical or even metaphysical dimension. In Heaney's terminology, the poetry, in varying ways, includes a sense of both 'place' and 'displacement'.[12] The interpenetration of the two is nowhere more apparent than in the work of Paul Muldoon; and it may well be that in him the Irish rural theme is advanced in poetry to a point of no return. His home place, Armagh—deciduous, apple-orcharded, and mushroomy, but also scene of some of the worst atrocities after 1968—is the location of all kinds of transformation and metamorphosis: in one poem's title the place-name 'Armagh' is itself dislocated into 'Armageddon, Armageddon'. Despite the various kinds of emblematic use Heaney makes of places like Broagh and Anahorish, a relish for the actual location persists, whereas Muldoon's Moy is a much less tangible, more fluidly combinative place. It is a place in which the father's mushroom farming dissolves into the son's eating of hallucinogenic mushrooms; in which rural patterns of life seem Native American rather than Irish; in which the Moy itself may suddenly crack apart into Marengo.

Yet, persistent beneath the surface of all these transformations are certain elements of a very specifically Irish rural heritage. A crucial one is an intimacy with the cultural and psychological effects of dissatisfaction and emigration. Muldoon's work is characteristically full of departures; and 'Why Brownlee Left', from the volume of that title published in 1980, is one of his paradigmatic poems. Brownlee, the ploughman whose name virtually defines him in terms of his function, has made his bid for freedom in a mysterious disappearance. In that disappearing trick the poem may be thought to mark the final disappearance in Irish rural poetry of that idealized image of the ploughman to be found in poems such as Padraic Colum's 'Plougher'. This is a ploughman saying goodbye to all that, a peasant turning tail on his 'little lyrical fields'. Brownlee has gone, we may imagine, to inherit Patrick Maguire's 'dawn in the year of One':

> By noon Brownlee was famous;
> They had found all abandoned, with
> The last rig unbroken, his pair of black
> Horses, like man and wife,
> Shifting their weight from foot to
> Foot, and gazing into the future.

3. Broken Worlds

During the 1930s and 1940s Kavanagh's mood of corrective deconstruction was mirrored in the work of a number of prose-writers. In particular, the Irish short story, in the hands of Sean O'Faolain (who founded the acerbically unorthodox journal *The Bell* in 1940) and Frank O'Connor, becomes the mode of an exploration of Irish rural and provincial life unillusioned in its attitudes to the self-approbatory sentimentalities, hypocrisies, and occlusions of post-revolutionary Ireland. In his shrewd study of the short story, *The Lonely Voice* (1965), O'Connor remarks on its special appropriateness to an Ireland in which the social complexity necessary to the novel has been so lacking. The short story focuses on what he calls 'submerged population groups' and 'outlawed figures wandering about the fringes of society'.[13] The lonely voices of the socially unintegrated may offer very valuable testimony to the alienating social structures they inhabit. The birth of the Free State in a time of insurrectionary violence, revolutionary idealism, and ambivalently contaminated emotions and impulses is the originary moment of creativity in both of these writers, as it is also in Liam O'Flaherty. The definitive texts of that story are O'Faolain's first collection, *Midsummer Night Madness* (1932), O'Connor's *Guests of the Nation* (1931), and O'Flaherty's novel *The Assassin* (1928). The disillusionment which followed on that origin, as Irish provincial life degenerated into stifling conventionality, repression, and hypocrisy, and as writers had to cope with the judgements of the Censorship Board, is the sustaining atmosphere in the work of O'Faolain and O'Connor and the ground of the frustrated idealism which O'Flaherty attempts to counter with a celebration of natural vigour and vitality.

Sean O'Faolain's stories are therefore much preoccupied with relationships between tradition and modernity, authoritarianism and spontaneity, repression and release in Irish life, particularly as they figure in, or are filtered through Catholicism. The short story, he says in his autobiography *Vive Moi!*, 'is pure essentialism',[14] and some of the best of his own stories discover poised, lucid, quasi-poetic figures or emblems through which the tensions and ambivalences of various positions are articulated and explored. 'The Silence of the Valley', for instance, plots the traditional Irish rural wake of a *seanachie* or story-teller in Co. Cork against a conversation about the future of Ireland held by a group of well-travelled sophisticates; and the story culminates in a moment of surprising recognition and complicity, below the level of intellectual debate, between a rural priest and an American soldier. 'The Sugawn Chair', almost a short prose-poem, ironizes, in the figure of a 'sugawn' or rope chair lying abandoned in an attic, the way rural skills and crafts have been lost by a newly urbanized class, despite a persistent, value-laden attachment to them which may easily corrode into the sentimental. 'A Broken World' sets three representative types in a railway train journeying through the Irish countryside to Dublin: the narrator (an intellectual and an *alter ego* for O'Faolain), a priest, and a farmer. The priest tells a story of two opposed kinds of Irish life, rural plenitude and rural poverty—cultural and spiritual as well as material. When the priest leaves the train, the narrator notices how sycophantically and obsequiously he is treated by everyone he passes on the platform. Subsequently he learns from the almost moronically unconcerned and uninterested farmer that the priest has been 'silenced' by the Church for his former political radicalism. The story concludes with the train approaching Dublin and the narrator gazing out onto a snowy scene: 'I could not deny to the wintry moment its own truth, and that under that white shroud, covering the whole of Ireland, life was lying broken and hardly breathing.' This image of the snow covering Ireland is inherited from the famous closing passage of Joyce's long short story 'The Dead', where the snow acts, in part, as a correlative for the emotionally frozen or smothered existence of the story's central character, Gabriel Conroy; and it is explicitly opposed in O'Faolain's story by the desire for an 'image of life that would fire and fuse us all', together with the certain knowledge of the hopelessness of this desire. The potential and desirable Irish community which might have been emblematized by having intellectual, priest and farmer harmoniously reconciled in the railway carriage is splintered into their various solitudes as they depart from the train and as we witness them arrested into immobile social and intellectual attitudes.

'A Broken World', then, supplies a rich emblem for the inertia of Irish cultural and intellectual life and for the institutional freezing and framing of people into the only roles this society will permit them. Again and again in O'Faolain's work, throughout a very long career, Ireland is imaged as such a 'broken world', its characters desiring spontaneity but suffering repression, looking for political or spiritual satisfaction but enduring abjection and disconsolation, desiring to live in the present but being compelled into retrospect, nostalgia, and fantasy (notably in the extraordinary and experimental story of marital unhappiness, 'The Woman Who Married Clark Gable' and what it calls the '*da capo*' of the existence it describes). The ambivalences explored in his work frequently turn on encounters between sexuality and Catholic doctrine, with the ensuing disintegrative psychological damage of guilt. It is this tension that makes 'Lovers of the Lake' one of his most memorable stories. Here a guilty married woman makes a pilgrimage to Lough Derg, that site of Catholic penitential expiation, where she is unexpectedly joined by her lover; and the lough becomes a figurative 'deep lake of human unhappiness'. At the end of the story the lovers go to a hotel together, but to separate bedrooms; and if what we have read here is in one clear sense an account of the psychopathology of mid-century Irish Catholic sexuality, it is an account managed with a full sense of the actualities of moral decision and their various complexities of hesitation and scruple. It is, therefore, an account which uncondescendingly gives its due to the confessional and penitential consolations of Catholicism. As a result, it is an exemplary instance of the humane, generously empathetic, but nevertheless disenchantedly ironizing intelligence to be discovered in the work of O'Faolain who, as he observes of the character called simply 'the Celt' in 'The Silence of the Valley', 'labours to resolve his own contradictions' in the form of the short story.

Frank O'Connor's stories share with O'Faolain's an inspection of Irish provincial life, and sometimes a specific Cork setting, but they tend to be less emblematic and more openly discursive. Indeed, a tone of relaxed conversational ease is the mode of address in many of them, and they frequently use a range of voices in dialogue and self-communion. Combined with this, however, is a strong sense of archetypal patterning in which the anecdotal may be deepened into the tragic. In *The Lonely Voice* O'Connor offers the theory that this is a typical feature of the short story when he says that its outlawed figures are 'superimposed sometimes on symbolic figures whom they caricature and echo—Christ, Socrates, Moses'.[15] These large shades behind

his own outlaws—priests, servant girls, IRA men, British soldiers, unhappily married women, frustrated intellectuals—lend
them pathos and dignity. In the superb title story of his first
collection, *Guests of the Nation* (1931), an extremely reluctant
IRA execution squad is ordered to kill its English hostages in
reprisal for the British Army's execution of a number of IRA
volunteers. In a touch of consummately chilling irony, O'Connor
has revealed the sympathetic matiness between IRA volunteers
and hostages before we—and they—learn of the impending execution. The hostages, therefore, who learn that they are to die
only at the last moment, initially think it a joke; but the chaotic
mess of the execution itself is transformed into an almost
Yeatsian symbolic moment when one of the men, the hitherto
silent Belcher, reveals Christ-like qualities of self-sacrifice, courage, and forgiveness. The final sentences of the story trace the
effect of the execution on its narrator, a participant: 'I was
somehow very small and lost and lonely like a child astray in the
snow. And anything that happened to me afterwards, I never felt
the same about again.'

The Irish inflection of the word 'astray', and the fractured
cadence of that last sentence, perfectly evoke the intense isolation and privacy of this consciousness. Such subjectivities are not
uncommon in O'Connor, even where the situations are less
extreme than they are in his stories of the Troubles. Priests
figure prominently in them, partly since he is fascinated, in such
stories as 'Uprooted' and 'A Mother's Warning', by their sexual
frustration and loneliness, but also because clerical celibacy is
read as a deeply inhibiting condition for Irish society more generally as well as for the individual isolated priest. In the disturbing, even nauseating story 'News for the Church', for instance, a
young woman's uninhibited, hearty sexual realism is corrupted,
in the confessional, by a priest's sadistically intrusive misogyny.
As in O'Faolain, however, O'Connor's critique of Irish Catholicism can also accommodate a sense of the potential heroism of
the priesthood: in 'Peasant' the priest's moral absolutism stands
over against the hypocritical complicities of his community—
although, in a typical piece of O'Connor irony, the priest is

broken by his battle, whereas the community survives and prospers in its venality.

More commonly, however, Church and state, represented by individual priests and policemen, are complicit agents of manipulation and control in the provincial Ireland of these stories, where religious affiliation triumphs over love, snobbery over spontaneity, decorum over passion, and, in one of the most heartbreaking of all his tales, 'The Mad Lomasneys', hysterical errors of judgement over the impulses of true feeling. The awful foreclosure of human happiness which results is O'Connor's abiding preoccupation. In one of his finest stories, 'A Story by Maupassant', the foreclosure, which leads to alcoholism and dissolution, is the result of intellectual ambition thwarted by pettiness, conventional piety, and the hypocritical corruption of the Church-dominated Irish educational system. The story turns on its hero's discovering, in his dissolution, the value of the work of Maupassant which, in youthful arguments with his friend— the story's narrator—he had once derided. The intertextuality of this reference is an acknowledgement by O'Connor himself of his mentors in the art of the short story. In this, it is not unlike the audacious way O'Faolain opens 'The Woman Who Married Clark Gable', about a Dublin woman, with the sentences, 'She should have lived in Moscow. If she had been a Russian she would have said . . .', which of course serves as a nod to O'Faolain's own mentors, Chekhov and Turgenev. If the ennui of pre-revolutionary Russia and the moral turpitude of nineteenth-century Paris seem appropriate points of comparison for post-revolutionary Ireland in the works of O'Faolain and O'Connor, these intertextual occasions may also be read now as testimony to their own achievements in the form of the short story. Inheriting their European models, and drawing on the Irish work of George Moore in *The Untilled Field* (1903), of Joyce in *Dubliners* (1914), and of Daniel Corkery in *A Munster Twilight* (1916), O'Faolain and O'Connor made the short story an essential vehicle for the representation of mid-century Irish provincial life.

Mary Lavin, whose first collection, *Tales from Bective Bridge*, was published in 1942, has a story called 'An Akoulina of the Irish Midlands' in which she places her work into a similarly intertextual orbit. The title alludes both to Turgenev's 'Hamlet of the Shchigrovsky District' and, as the story's narrator makes plain in its opening sentences, to another of his stories, 'The Tryst', in which a beautiful peasant girl, Akoulina, is cruelly and off-handedly jilted by her lover, Victor Alexandritch. The narrator of 'The Tryst' is the deeply sympathetic, recoiling Turgenev himself, *in propria persona*, since the story is one of his autobiographical *Sketches from a Hunter's Album*. As narrator, he presents himself overhearing the final conversation of the lovers while he takes shelter in a rain-soaked forest, and the story's final gesture is his retrieval from the forest's floor of Akoulina's pathetic nosegay of wild flowers.

Lavin's story alludes to the Turgenev in several ways. The Irish Akoulina, translated into a plain hotel maid called Lena, is overheard by the narrator in a forest tryst with her lover, the cabman Andy Hackett. The narrator's role hovers much more uncertainly and suspectly than Turgenev's between empathy and voyeurism; and the meeting of the lovers is not final but part of a process of seduction. Lena, a Protestant, has decided to convert to Catholicism in order to marry Hackett, and has brought with her to the wood the Catholic catechism given to her by her priest. Hackett, however, learning of her intention in the forest, is enraged: he wishes, from the depths of great loneliness, to retain amicable relations with Lena's family, and intends instead a pregnancy culminating in a marriage that Lena's parents will give their blessing to. The story ends with his guiding, or compelling, a vaguely resisting Lena into the undergrowth, and with the narrator's comparing the catechism, which Hackett has taken from her and torn to pieces, to Akoulina's nosegay.

Mary Lavin's intertextuality is very sly here. Turgenev's story, with its gentle and tactful generosity to the peasantry, was read in its own day as deeply subversive of the Tsarist social system. Lavin, whose work lacks the satirical animus and analytic edge of O'Faolain and O'Connor, nevertheless insinuates in this story the entrapment of contemporary Irish characters, particularly women, in a deeply disadvantageous social system too—in this case in the absurdities of sectarian exclusivity. From *Tales of Bective Bridge* until her death in 1995, Mary Lavin continued to produce work of distinction at precisely this level of subtlety and restraint. She scrupulously identifies an Irish rural and provincial world where 'charity is tempered with prudence' ('Sarah'), where 'poverty had the dignity of a lost cause well fought' ('Say Could That Lad Be I?'), where children are educated into 'the first bitter foretaste of human impotence' ('The Sand Castle'), where an almost surgical scrutiny is applied to the tensions and terrors of 'connubial privacy' ('A Tragedy'), and where, in 'At Sallygap', which is almost an extension, and gender inversion, of Joyce's 'Eveline' in *Dubliners*, a potential escape is thwarted by timorousness into a marriage in which the escapee is 'imprisoned for ever in hatred'. Lavin's best work, as a result, takes its rightful place beside that of O'Faolain and O'Connor as one of the crucial formative influences on the subsequent rich history of the Irish short story—a history which includes the work of Benedict Kiely, William Trevor, and John McGahern.

In Trevor, in particular, the form is given one of its most interesting contemporary extensions. The melancholy of his stories may derive, in part, from the legacy of O'Faolain and O'Connor, but it undoubtedly derives also from his origins in the lower-middle-class Protestant Irish provincial class. In the period following the War of Independence the effective social status of this class deteriorated rapidly, and Trevor's work, frequently set in the 1940s and 1950s, is alert to both the pathos and the farce of the way it is doomed to disintegration while still attempting to preserve, with increasing desperation, its sense of superiority. His interest in this class or caste is by no means exclusive in his work, which is in fact remarkable for its social and denominational range and for the punctiliousness of its tracing of economic actuality in rural and provincial Irish life; but he nevertheless charts this post-revolutionary demographic imperative with exceptional inwardness and sensitivity. The fading of the Protestant middle classes gives him his crucial theme: that is, the various ways, personal and cultural, in which the present may become dominated by, or entrapped in the past.

This preoccupation is the impulse behind his Big House novel, *Fools of Fortune*; but it also supplies the motive of one of his finest stories, the novella *Reading Turgenev*, published as the first half of *Two Lives* (1991). Mary Louise Dallon is about to be released, after thirty-one years, from a mental asylum into 'the community', in that cynical piece of late 1980s anti-social engineering; and the phases of her release are juxtaposed with the narrative of the emotional and sexual distresses which put her there. The victim of that period of Irish social history which made marriage between provincial Irish Protestants more and more difficult, as they emigrated in the wake of the founding of the new state, she chooses an entirely inappropriate, older partner unable to consummate their marriage. As a result, her own emotional life becomes dominated by her brief relationship with a sickly cousin, Robert; and his early death is the prelude to her long period of demented mourning and morbidity. Indeed, it is suggested that she wilfully chooses her 'insanity' out of the desire to sacrifice her life more intensely to his memory; and in this way it is possible to read her obsession as a moving into fatal melancholia of Gretta Conroy's fascination with the long-dead figure of her youthful lover Michael Furey in Joyce's story 'The Dead'. Any judgement on the social organization which makes for such abject thwartedness of desire remains implicit in Trevor's finely evocative, always descriptively realistic prose; but the subtleties of implicit judgement produce some of his finest effects, where the whole burden of the story is carried in its spare and simple phrasings. One such is the devastating understatement of the single sentence giving us Mary's courtship: 'the curiosity of affection was not present on either side.' The discipline of reticence here, in its controlled decorum, gives emotional abjection its due, with terrifying exactitude; and Trevor manages a comparable intensity in a wide range of stories, including the virtually paradigmatic 'The Ballroom of Romance' where, for the heroine Bridie, 'Tears were a luxury, like flowers would be in the fields where the marigolds grew, or fresh white-wash in the scullery'.

If *Reading Turgenev* and 'The Ballroom of Romance' offer personal histories trapped in social patterns, other stories of Trevor's, such as 'The Distant Past', 'The News from Ireland', and 'Beyond the Pale', present a more direct engagement with Irish political history. In 'The Distant Past' a Protestant couple from a Big House undergo, during their lives, a cycle of relation-ship with their Catholic neighbours in which initial alienation during the War of Independence turns into sympathetic post-revolutionary tolerance, and shifts back again into deep hostility after the return of the Troubles in 1968: 'Because of the distant past they would die friendless. It was worse than being murdered in their beds.' It is a story which exceptionally handles the effect of the Troubles on Southern communities too, where their im-pact on tourism is the mercenary impulse behind revised social relations. In 'The News from Ireland' an English governess's experiences in an Irish Big House during the nineteenth-century Famine is read, by the house's butler, as instinct with the entire scope of Anglo-Irish relations: the butler, Fogarty, so to say, dreams the Irish political future. And 'Beyond the Pale' restores the original political sense to the now usually figurative phrase of its title. The 'Pale' was the area around Dublin beyond which English rule did not extend, and therefore where the 'wild Irish' lived; and the story concerns an Englishwoman, Cynthia, on holiday in Co. Antrim who, herself deeply read in Irish history, fractures the smug serenity of her travelling companions when she describes her encounter with a young Irishman who, caught up in the Troubles, kills himself. There is possibly an element of the melodramatic and over-determined about this story; but it makes it plain how central to Trevor's sense of things is the contrast between the Irish and the English locations of his work: 'History is unfinished in this island; long since it has come to a stop in Surrey.' Which itself needs to be corrected only in insist-ing that, of course, in so far as it is 'unfinished in this island', it is also, and always, unfinished in Surrey too, loath as Surrey may be to admit it: and this is what Cynthia knows.

4. Puritan Ireland

In some of its plots Trevor's work maintains a continuity with the impulses behind O'Faolain's and O'Connor's, even if his stories have actually been written in the period defined by John Montague's Yeatsian refrain in his poem 'The Siege of Mullingar', published as part of *The Rough Field* in 1972: 'Puritan Ireland's dead and gone, | A myth of O'Connor and O'Faolain'. In fact, some of the most significant novels and plays after, as well as before, the 1960s have been much preoccupied with the 'puritan' moment of the Irish mid-century. These texts would appear to indicate that Montague was either too sanguine, or possibly intended an irony, in his otherwise rather over-eager epitaph. Some imaginings of rural and provincial places define and identify this moment with great intensity and clarity, and often with a strong historical sense, in ways that make for a kind of revelatory literary topography in modern Irish writing. In one of his poems Tom Paulin speaks of 'theoretical locations'; and all of these places may be so regarded. They are places of the imagination, spaces which are also ideas, instinct with a moral or political significance, places where various issues raised by the real place of Ireland may be opened up and explored. Such places would include Kate O'Brien's 'Mellick', her literary version of Limerick; John McGahern's and Edna O'Brien's anonymous small towns, villages, and farms of the West and the Midlands; Brian Friel's 'Ballybeg', an apparently actual, but unmapped place in his imaginatively realized Co. Donegal; Tom Murphy's fictional western village of 'Bailegangaire'; and Colm Toibin's seaside village of Cush, in Co. Wexford, a landscape having prominent associations with the rebellion of the United Irishmen in 1798.

In Kate O'Brien's novels of the 1930s and 1940s, notably *The Ante-Room* (1934), *The Land of Spices* (1941), and *The Last of Summer* (1943), she creates a fictional setting, Mellick, out of the city and environs of her native provincial city, Limerick. The social world of her novels, which otherwise features only very rarely in Irish writing, is that of the Catholic upper middle classes, the inhabitants of Big Houses and select convent schools.[16] Her subject is essentially the private one of love and friendship, but all three of these books contextualize their material in the politics of a class insecure in its origins and, as a result, clinging to its privilege against any threat to the *status quo*, whether that of Parnell in the 1880 of *The Ante-Room*, the clamour for independence in the pre-1916 period in *The Land of Spices*, or the unthinkingly self-congratulatory support for a policy of neutrality as the Second World War approaches in *The Last of Summer*. It is also a society religious in ways that combine genuine piety with queasy pietism, spiritual striving with mercenary worldliness. O'Brien's plotting of her characters' relationships into this world is managed with an insight and tact in which affectionate recognition shades off into satiric rebuke, sympathetic involvement into a strong sense of the ridiculous, and in which a conception of individual bravery and nobility of mind must contend with an account of petty snobbery and pretension. If these are Jamesian themes—and James's *Washington Square* is referred to several times in *The Ante-Room*—they are handled by O'Brien in ways that make 'Mellick' a central location on the map of modern Irish writing, a fictional topography charted with great imaginative accuracy. Within it she inspects and experimentally explores the degree to which her characters—men as well as women, but particularly women—both internalize and resist, or turn to some alternative profit, the social forms and conventions they inherit.

That O'Brien uses the fictional name Mellick, and that *The Ante-Room* and *The Land of Spices* are historical novels, suggests both the kind of distancing perspective she requires for her work and also the means by which she attempted to circumvent the restrictions of the Censorship Board, which would have been impossible had some of her themes had a contemporary 1930s or 1940s setting. (She did, nevertheless, like almost all the good writers of the period, fall foul of the Board, and her novels regularly appeared on the Index of Censored Publications.) These narrative structures are complemented by the use of an outsider figure—the English, Belgian-educated Reverend Mother in *The Land of Spices*, the French niece of an Irish Big House in *The Last of Summer*—as a means of judging or, indeed, rebuking post-revolutionary Irish complacencies and self-mythologizings. In *The Land of Spices* we see the Irish through the nun's un-illusioned perspective: 'They were an ancient, martyred race, and of great importance to themselves—that meagre handful of conceptions made a history, made a problem—and made them at once unconquerable and a little silly.' And the outsider Angèle in *The Last of Summer* reads in the Irish 'an arrogance of austerity, contempt for personal feeling, coldness and perhaps fear of idiosyncracy'. These rebukes are utterly uningratiating in their decided and edgy resistance to certain Irish stereotypes and self-conceptions; and O'Brien's plots are coolly located against these perceived failures in human warmth and empathy.

The Ante-Room is set in a Catholic Big House, Roseholm, over three crucial feast days of the Catholic Church, the Eve and Feast of All Saints and the Feast of All Souls, as the mother of the house lies dying. The plot turns on the illicit but unconsummated love between Agnes Mulqueen, the daughter of the house, and Vincent, her brother-in-law. Agnes's Catholic crisis of conscience impels her rejection of Vincent, the consequence of which is his suicide and her projected marriage to a man she admires but does not love. The novel takes no sides in her decision; but the struggle of conscience itself, and the psychological reality of belief, are very sensitively conveyed. *The Ante-Room* is a novel as good on the psychology of an earlier form of Catholicism as the work of François Mauriac in France, although it replaces his Jansenist gloom with a more inwardly sympathetic sense of the way the religion may mediate or even salve some of the most intractable human distresses.

In the figure of Agnes's uncle, Canon Considine, *The Ante-Room* includes a convincing portrayal of a certain kind of materialistic but nevertheless virtuous upper-middle-class Irish priest. The combination has been an unexceptional one in Irish social life, but infrequent in Irish writing, although there are comparable instances in some of the work of George Moore and Canon Sheehan. O'Brien's fascination with the complex entanglements of the religious life in the mercenary or venal quotidian existences of the Irish Catholic *bourgeoisie* is written large in *The Land of Spices*. Here the Catholic Big House is transposed into that other big house with which it has had such a deeply reciprocal relationship, the convent school, in this case that of the French religious order of the *Compagnie de la Sainte Famille*; and the novel consequently goes, as it were, psychologically as well as spatially inside the walls of the religious institution so influential on this class and its culture. At the centre of the book is the relationship between the convent's Reverend Mother, Mère Marie-Hélène (the previous Helen Archer), and a pupil, Anna Murphy, daughter of a Catholic Big House, as it develops through the latter's brilliant scholastic career. Both are intellectuals, although they are given very different choices and opportunities. However, they also share the fact that they are both to some degree maimed by their fathers: Helen by the homosexuality of hers—her discovery of this is the reason for her entering the convent—and Anna by the alcoholism and dissipation of hers.

The subtly feminist portrayal of this relationship is, then, one which includes deep psycho-sexual trauma as well as the charting of developing intellectual opportunity. Helen's cosmopolitan argument with the obscurantism of Irish Catholicism—her internationalism against their nationalism—is balanced against the culturally conditioned hysteria of her discovery of her father's sexuality; Anna's fight to attend university is predicated on Helen's heroic argument in favour of it with the girl's repressive family. The novel's partly sublimated, partly explicitated preoccupation with homosexual love, which is read as both inhibition and ultimate enablement, draws its two heroines into complementarity. In focusing O'Brien's crucial theme of the 'secret life' of the psyche, or of what she is unafraid to call the 'soul', which must make its way in a social world at best indifferent and at worst, and more usually, hostile to its delicacies and hesitations, the novel also plots a handing on of rights from one generation of women to another. This is managed quite without sentimentality or strain at a time when the expression of such things was particularly difficult for an Irish Catholic woman, and in a way that gives uncustomary credit to the conventual educational system of Catholicism which, however repressive, also supplies such opportunity.

This ability of O'Brien's derives from the combination in her of a brave psychoanalytical radicalism with what appears a theologically relatively orthodox Catholicism. She understands both psychological and cultural systems of tradition, of handing-on and continuity, in ways that avoid the simplistic, the craven, and the modish. This is notably the case when she provides us with Helen's gradual coming to terms with her father's sexuality in *The Land of Spices*. Her earlier terrified contraction and withdrawal flowers into a loving understanding that 'a soul should not take upon itself the impertinence of being frightened for another soul'. This lesson in humility is a richly humanist radicalization of dogmatic turn-of-the-century Catholicism, a kind of Jamesianly subtleized version of it; and its expression constitutes a central moment in the history of the modern Irish novel.

In the work of Edna O'Brien something of Kate O'Brien's feminism and sexual exploratoriness persists into a later generation of Irish women's writing. If Edna O'Brien lacks Kate O'Brien's vigorous stylistic signature—her work can sometimes seem stylistically almost invisible or inaudible—the trilogy of the early 1960s, *The Country Girls* (1960), *Girl with Green Eyes* (1962), and *Girls in their Married Bliss* (1964)—together with *A Pagan Place* (1970), retain their power to convince and shock as authoritative representations of characteristic Irish rural transitions in the period of their composition. They chart the movements of Irish women from a culturally and economically depleted rural West to Dublin and thence to London; from singleness to marriage, children, divorce, and a difficult, barely sustainable economic and social independence; from inadequate educational opportunity to the discovery of channels for the expression of literary ambition; and from the dominating and oppressive forms of an inherited Catholicism to a secularity nevertheless still haunted by the old paternal and authoritarian repressions. Through the joint heroines of the trilogy, Kate Brady and Baba Brennan, O'Brien gives expression to a common Irish destiny with a brave panache which still makes it easy to see why her books were not only banned but burned in the Ireland of their first publication. Their patterns of domestic drunkenness and sexlessness, of Church hypocrisy and sexual hysteria—frequently occluded by an opportunistic pietism—are commandingly expressed. Kate Brady is a close reader of Joyce; and in key passages of her early work Edna O'Brien has clearly been enabled by Joyce in the expression of a sexuality not ribald so much as plain-spoken, owning to and knowing the danger of its own cultural distinctiveness, unafraid to record the sometimes frightful negativity of Irish women's sexual relations with men:

I thought of all the women who had it and didn't even know when the big moment was, and others saying their Rosary with the beads held over the side of the bed . . . and it often leading to nothing and them getting up out of bed and riding a poor doorknob and kissing the wooden face of a door and urging with foul language, then crying, wiping the knob, and it all adding up to nothing either.[17]

If the rhythms and bravado of Molly Bloom persist in this monologue of Baba's in *Girls in their Married Bliss*, the negativity and sexual despair are her own; and the representation of such 'nothingness' is Edna O'Brien's permanent contribution to contemporary Irish prose.

John McGahern's Midlands is notably defined in both his short stories and his novels. In three of the latter, in particular, he expresses a developing and complex set of attitudes in realistic narratives which deepen into quasi-allegorical resonance: *The Barracks* (1963), *The Dark* (1965), and *Amongst Women* (1990).[18] These are intensely claustrophobic domestic fictions set in unnamed small-farm country, and all three focus on the family relationships of difficult, violent fathers with their wives and children: the guard (policeman) Reegan in *The Barracks*, whose

career, after fighting for the IRA during the War of Independence, is a disillusioned failure to secure a good position in the
subsequent jockeying for power, and whose wife Elizabeth
slowly dies during the course of the book; the small farmer
Mahoney in *The Dark*; and Moran in *Amongst Women*, who has
also been a member of the IRA but who refuses in disgust to
draw a pension from it, repudiating the post-Independence culture of 'pull'. McGahern's prose is a limpid development of the
'scrupulous meanness' of Joyce's *Dubliners*, that style attuned to
deep personal and cultural depression, whose realism is capable
of sudden vivid fractures into depths of both lyrical plangency
and stomach-turning disgust. Its elegance therefore acts as an
almost obsessive intensification of McGahern's themes of domestic violence, sexual and emotional repression, bodily and
cultural decay; and its slow deliberateness is an exact mirror of
the undifferentiated post-revolutionary Irish stasis of which it
offers a dejected analysis.

In *The Barracks* the embittered policeman Reegan sustains a
sullenly combative relationship with his superintendent, whom
he regards as a representative of the newly venal and mercenary
Ireland which has succeeded the heroically transformative moment of such men as Reegan himself, and an affectionate but
unforthcoming relationship with his wife. Elizabeth Reegan is
the first of McGahern's characteristically sensitive depictions of
Irish women. Isolated, returned home after a nursing career in
London, bookish when she gets the chance, she is literally dying
in the police-barracks of the novel's title in this post-war rural
Ireland; but the literal death is figuratively congruent with the
country's cultural depredations. Among these, the daily round
of Catholicism, with its patronizing, interfering, and bullying
priests, is manifestly the crucial one; and the mournful dirge of
the family rosary, which frequently punctuates with irony scenes
of domestic tension and brutality, acts as an image of deep
abjection, shackling the family in its monotonously circular and
dolorous chain. We are presumably intended to read out of the
book's title a view of post-revolutionary rural Ireland as itself
constriction and confinement, a nation which has replaced the

'barracks' of the British Army with that of the new state's civil power and the Church's ecclesiastical jurisdiction. Reegan himself reads the Irish flag which flies over the police depot in the Phoenix Park in Dublin as a measure of the difference between his once-revolutionary 'dream' of Ireland and the present disintegration of that dream, seeing 'the fault in the strip of green and gold with the white between . . . symbolizing the institution of Eire'. McGahern's portrayal of Elizabeth's lucid interiority, set against these constrictions, constitutes a poignant ode to the frustrated desire for a fulfilling love—of nation as well as wife.

Where Elizabeth Reegan's chances of another life are all locked into the past and her long-gone relationship with a nihilistic but supportively educated English lover, those of the motherless boy hero of *The Dark* are yet to be discovered in a future; and where the violence of Reegan's nature is characteristically repressed, in Mahoney, the father of this novel, it is hideously explicit. The novel opens with what is arguably—and there are some contenders—the most frightful scene in modern Irish fiction, when Mahoney orders his son to strip naked and, in front of his sister, to undergo an elaborately sadistic ritual of threatened beating—the equivalent of a kind of phoney execution—during which he urinates in terror. The child is also, as we subsequently learn, the victim of his father's sexual abuse in their shared bed ('shame and embarrassment and loathing, the dirty rags of intimacy'). In these contexts of familial dominance and submission, 'the dark' of the title takes on various connotations. It is the dark of the lavatory to which the child retreats for his unique opportunity of solitude; of the bedroom in which he guiltily masturbates; of the confessional in which he experiences humiliation and shame; of the presbytery surrounded by the dead in which he stays with a priest cousin of the family (who also makes sexual advances) while trying to decide whether to become a priest himself; of his longing for what his feverish inexperience imagines as the 'savage darkness' of women; and, finally, of rural Irish hatred and self-pity, that obscuring and obscurantist darkness through which all of McGahern's characters must fumble their way. It is remarkable how tellingly and presciently McGahern illuminates these darknesses decades in advance of current revelations about domestic and ecclesiastical child abuse in Irish society.

This *Bildungsroman* leaves its hero unnamed and oscillates between first-, second-, and third-person narrative. As a result, it invites readings both autobiographical and generic: this life, if it is close to McGahern's own, his *Portrait of the Artist as a Young Man*, is also a representative one of its time and place. The repressed, timorous son must contest the brutality of the father to win through to the possibility of an alternative future. The battle is engaged through education, the stark alternatives being university or emigration. The novel's plot of educational opportunity is, however, a very damaged arc, since this child, having won the freedom of a university scholarship, rejects it for a safer civil service job. In McGahern, high ambition and achievement are always poisoned into under-achievement and the second best: the glimmerings of light are obscured in other kinds of semi-darkness. Finding an appropriate language for this, McGahern's prose accommodates a sadly flattened, almost Beckettian poignancy: 'But why had things to happen as they did, why could there not be some happiness, it'd be as easy.'

In *Amongst Women* the father, Moran—who has also appeared earlier in some of McGahern's short stories—is almost another version of Mahoney, intellectually and emotionally thwarted, but viewed now through the perspectives of familial retrospect. Beginning and ending in the present tense of the old man's last illness, the novel is mainly taken up with reminiscences of his behaviour towards, and effect on his children, who have variously grown, left home, emigrated to England, and married. A violent incident very like the one described at the beginning of *The Dark* has set his son Luke in permanent estrangement from him in London; but his other four children are both drawn to, and repelled by their father and the farm of their childhood on which he still lives, Great Meadow. The novel's retrospective structure allows McGahern to reveal the extent to which the children of a violent and dominant Irish father recreate his image in their subsequent lives, to the advantage of some

but to the disablement of others. He shows how they may release themselves from their past or be permanently sucked back
into an imaginatively idealized or heroized version of it, particularly from the distance of English exile. In this way, Great
Meadow with its old, disillusioned, embittered Republican
owner may be read as a symbol for rural Ireland itself, and the
portrayal of 'that larger self of family'—a word constantly on
Moran's lips—as a version of the nation. In *Amongst Women* the
children of the new state are seen in relationships of servitude
to, entrapment by, and dependency on it, and take their chances
of potential rejection, escape, or accommodation.

As its title suggests, the novel focuses most attention on the
way the daughters of the family, together with Moran's second
wife Rose, manage Moran's will to dominance and the intransi-
gent masculinism of the culture from which it derives. In managing Moran, they also expose the vulnerability and self-pity in
which masculine violence originates, bringing into full relief in
McGahern's work what is only implicit in *The Barracks* and *The
Dark*. In *Amongst Women* the negative judgements of the domestic and social repercussions of Irish masculinism meet a
richly historical contextualizing of it which understands it, for
instance, as the displaced repression of a long Irish rural history
in which the terror of workhouse and famine are constants.
Moran is, as a result, McGahern's most complex creation, and
the struggle of his daughters his most intensely dramatized plot.
The novel explores the deep structures of the routine and the
quotidian as the daughters move from their childhood inability
to do other than 'bend' to Moran's will, through their knowing,
after his second marriage, that, together with Rose, 'they were
mastered and yet they were controlling together what they were
mastered by', up to the old man's dying days in which, for the
first time in his life, he is frightened of them. These tense relationships of familial power are handled in the book in a way that
leaves no doubt that they are also intense relationships of familial love. The novel is a fine study of how love and power are both
collusive and antagonistic in traditional patterns of Irish domestic life. When Moran says, as he does more than once, that 'No

one is ever lost to the family unless they want to be', his saying is ambivalently inflected with both generosity and threat.

The real triumph in the book is ultimately that of the daughter, Sheila. Ensuring that her own children do not suffer the diminished expectations which Moran encouraged in her, she wins her final attitude from the purposive strength of her own will and intelligence, as she reorganizes patterns of obligation into voluntariness, of servitude into self-reliance. Her victory may be regarded as a climactic moment of enablement not only in the frequently depressed work of John McGahern but in the history of Irish rural writing: 'She would belong to the family but not on any terms. She knew instinctively that she could not live without it: she would need it, she would use it, but she would not be used by it except in the way she wanted.'

In Brian Friel's plays of Irish rural life retrospect is also a familiar perspective, often supported by non-realistic, experimental dramatic structures and forms. In *Philadelphia, Here I Come!* (1965) the central character, Gar, oppressed by Irish small-town life and by a boorish father, and about to emigrate, is split into a public and a private self, played by different actors, so that his alienation is dramatized as a virtual schizophrenia enforced by his domestic and cultural circumstances; and in *The Loves of Cass Maguire* (1966) Cass, returned from America to a home which utterly fails to match her retrospective fantasizing of it, directly addresses the audience and insists on giving her version of events: so that what we witness on stage is, partly, her reconstruction. In such ways Friel dramatizes not only the constrictions of rural life themselves, but the way they are meditated on and transformed in the future lives of his characters: his is very much a theatre of loss, memory, haunting, and the desperate desire for restoration which may always collapse into the entrapping tropes of nostalgia.

Philadelphia, Here I Come! is, like several of Friel's plays, including (as we saw in Chapter 1) the historical play *Translations*, set in the fictional location of 'Ballybeg', in the real county of Donegal. ('Ballybeg' means literally 'small town'.) The area of Ballybeg is turned in the light of Friel's constant and maturing dramatic scrutiny to reveal numerous different facets of its emotional, cultural, and political being, through its sometimes mutually exclusive social strata: the *petite bourgeoisie* in *Philadelphia*; the decayed upper-class Catholics of the local Big House, Ballybeg Hall, in *Aristocrats* (1979); the moneyed Dublin politicos who restore the place's thatched cottages as weekend and holiday homes in *The Communication Cord* (1982). One of Friel's richest explorations of the place, however, and one of his most inventive theatrical structures, is *Dancing at Lughnasa* (1990), in which singing and dancing are used almost as they are in some of the work of Dennis Potter: as, that is to say, the register of quite other orders of being and awareness from those the characters display in their ordinary existences.

Retrospection in this play is structurally conveyed by having the child character, Michael, present only imaginatively in the scenes in which he figures, but actually present on stage as the narrator-commentator looking back on these experiences from the perspective of his young manhood. The play thus presents us simultaneously with the event and the significance of the event in the story of a life. The effect is both commanding and full of pathos, as we watch through his own self-perception the influences formatively at work on this child. *Dancing at Lughnasa* is, we might say, an exact theatrical record of the Wordsworthian process through which the child becomes father to the man. The story is set in Ballybeg in August 1936 (the year of de Valera's re-election as Taoiseach, prime minister); and the political events of the time (de Valera's election itself, Mussolini's campaign in Abyssinia, the Spanish Civil War, memories of the Irish War of Independence) are often at least at the edge of earshot in the play. The narrator, Michael, is the illegitimate son of one of the five sisters of the Mundy family; and the story he tells in the play sets these sisters, and their brother, a priest sent home for 'going native' after twenty-five years as an African missionary, in their defining and confining social circumstances. In the midst of this larger political history, the locale of Ballybeg is undergoing its own belated industrial revolution also as a result of de Valera's policies ('Let them build a factory in every hamlet'), with the arrival of a knitwear factory which destroys the livelihood of two of the sisters. This is a Ballybeg, and a rural Ireland, therefore, at a transitional point in its history; and it could well be that the play's title draws ironically on that idealizing speech of de Valera's which I have already cited, which also famously includes a vision of 'comely maidens dancing at the crossroads'.

Lughnasa—Irish for the month of August—is the ancient feast of the Celtic god of harvest, Lugh, traditionally celebrated with sacrificial rituals and abandoned dancing. The pagan ceremony persists in the back hills of Ballybeg in 1936; but in the village itself the celebration is reduced to the annual harvest dance which Kate, the eldest sister, will not allow the others to attend. However, the ritual dance of Lughnasa does persist in the play in several senses. Jack, the priest brother, has become an initiate of mystery cults while a missionary in Uganda, and some of both the play's humour and its sadness derive from his descriptions of his involvement in, and attachment to the African ceremonial. When he dances alone while remembering the pagan rite, he insists that 'in some respects they're not unlike us'. The sisters have an alternative pagan deity: the intermittently working wireless which some of them want to christen 'Lugh', but which in fact they call simply 'Marconi'; and this fickle god of the airwaves acts on them very much as the pagan ceremonial acts on their brother. In the popular dance music and the Irish traditional music which comes to them through 'Marconi's voodoo' the sisters are transformed into dervishes, dancing away for a moment, in a display and a self-display that is both moving and grotesque (and also deeply exhilarating for an audience), the social, cultural, and sexual desolation of their lives. The Lughnasa dance becomes, then, a rich symbol for Dionysiac, hedonistic transformation and disruption in the timid hesitation and sexual unease of rural Irish Catholicism in the 1930s, and also for the persistence (in an Ireland about to inherit the forms of modern industrial society) of ancient patterns of emotional self-definition. During the course of the play, as we watch the world of the Mundy sisters disintegrate, leaving two of them destitute emigrants in England and another a deeply unhappy factory labourer, the dance becomes the dreamlike register of a space of female empowerment and definition, the figure for a solidarity and release nowhere else available to them in the ordinary social world of their time.

Despite the play's tragic dimension, however, Michael's final speech is, in one precise sense, hopeful. Like the daughters of Moran in *Amongst Women* discovering their own ways of becoming their father, and therefore of inventing themselves newly for an alternative future, Michael has taken fully into himself an understanding of his mother's and aunts' Lughnasa dance. This enables him to articulate their inarticulacy: 'as if this ritual, this wordless ceremony, was now the way to speak, to whisper private and sacred things, to be in touch with some otherness . . . Dancing as if language no longer existed because words were no longer necessary . . .' In the forms of Friel's own play he has found a way of articulating this inarticulate grief, subjection, and desire. In the character of Michael, and his masculine understanding of this female dance form, the play uncovers an image for the way a personality may become independently self-assured without condescending to the victims of the old defeats and constraints. Michael—character, narrator, and commentator—therefore represents a heritage embraced and transformed, an illegitimacy making its own laws.

Forms of experimentation in Friel are matched in the theatre of Tom Murphy by extraordinary combinations, juxtapositions, and transgressions. His work is wide-ranging in its preoccupations and locations, but one major focus of interest remains the rural West of his childhood and upbringing. In a trio of plays first performed in 1985—*Conversations on a Homecoming*, *Bailegangaire*, and *A Thief of a Christmas*—he brings together, in characteristic fashion, elements of realism, folk-tale, and myth in ways that may properly be considered to have a metaphysical as well as an ethical dimension, turning on questions of social and cultural identity while also enquiring into the very possibility of authenticity and integrity. In *Conversations on a Homecoming* a pub in east Galway in the early 1970s becomes the apparently realistic setting for an examination of a rural Ireland suffering withdrawal from the false utopianism of the economic and cultural dream of the 1960s associated with the image and programme of the Irish-American President, John Fitzgerald Kennedy. In the play's own absent and now debased Kennedy-like figure, J.J., Murphy presents a potent and viable emblem for the god that failed; and the play, as the pub's name, 'The White House', first suggests, deepens its realism into metaphorical, symbolic, and allegorical resonance. Around the figure of J.J., who is endlessly discussed by the play's bar-flies as they get drunk together in an almost Sartrean confinement or claustrophobia (emphasized by the one-act structure),[19] various types of Irish rural distress and disillusionment, but also resilience, are defined, as the play's historical sense—reading the early 1970s from the perspective of the mid-1980s—registers the impact of Americanization, emigration, and return. In the play's acutely rendered dialogue the largest issues of the relations between Church and State, art and censorship, tradition and renewal, are debated in pub banter become increasingly edgy, acerbic, and aggressive.

In the related plays, *Bailegangaire* and *A Thief of a Christmas*, a historical perspective is more deeply embedded into the structure and fabric, in a way that reminds us that one of Murphy's earliest plays, *Famine* (1968), recovered the circumstances of the nineteenth-century Irish famine in vividly contemporary dramatic forms. In *Bailegangaire* an old woman, Mommo, in the kitchen of a thatched house in 1984, obsessively tells the story of a 'laughing contest' at Christmas time fifty years previously, in which one of the contestants died, and as a result of which a child was burnt to death in a fire. Mommo's astonishing monologue frequently uses both Irish and rich Irishisms in a way that makes it dense with a social and linguistic history without ever becoming picturesque or archaic. As the story progresses, in a regressive and repetitive manner, it becomes clear that Mommo is actually telling the story of her own experience; and she is telling it to her granddaughters, Mary and Dolly, the latter of whom is pregnant. Mommo is herself a central character in the story, the wife who encourages her husband, one of the contestants, to laugh at, or in the face of, 'misfortune': her encouragement is therefore a type of Promethean or Nietzschean defiance of the gods.

The second play, *A Thief of a Christmas*, is plotted around the ferocious contest itself and the almost demented gambling that accompanies it. The folkloric elements of the plays are pointed up by the subtitles, in which the first is described as 'The Story of Bailegangaire and how it came by its appellation' and the second as 'The Actuality of how Bailegangaire came by its appellation'. The plays define the way the place 'Bochtan' ('the poor place') became 'Bailegangaire' ('the place without laughter'); and, using a variety of experimental theatrical means, including music, prayer, and noise, their act of etymology, the folkloric uncovering of how places are named, is also a means of defining and recovering, in the present moment of the Irish mid-1980s, a tragic rural history, neither sentimentalized nor idealized, but inspected with the desire to comprehend, interiorize, and, possibly, make it usable as a form of future cultural mobility.

As Fintan O'Toole has shown,[20] the plays finely interweave the metaphysical and the actual, the folkloric and the socio-economic. Mommo's quasi-mythical narrative, which is a mother's story of her child's death—still so painful to her, after fifty years, that it has to be held at the arm's length of her third-person narrative—is both a tragic inversion of the Christmas story and one congruent with the public discourse of dead babies in the Irish mid-1980s (the debate about abortion, and the long, pathetic saga of the 'Kerry babies' case which involved infanticide), a discourse also alluded to in some of the misfortunes laughed at in *A Thief of a Christmas*, which include 'the unbaptised and still-born buried in unconsecrated ground . . . a field haunted by infants'. Similar convergences of different worlds in *Bailegangaire* include the fact that the play's thatched cottage is set in a landscape containing a multinational factory at which there is severe industrial unrest; and that Mommo and Mary are articulate, intelligent, and literary in ways at odds with those theatrical representations of Irish 'peasants' with which an audience might initially confuse them. In these transgressive interpenetrations Murphy finds theatrical forms adequate both to the recording of an Ireland which moved from the agricultural to the post-industrial with astonishing speed in the 1960s and 1970s, and to an interrogation of some deeply received images and emblems, those which also figured, very differently, in the theatre of the Irish Literary Revival. If Mommo is a version of Mother Ireland or Kathleen ni Houlihan, she is also a dominating, manipulative, senile old woman, a Shan van Vacht become a possessive and sterile matriarch. The matriarchy she represents is nevertheless one with which Mary, her granddaughter, must come to terms—and explicitly 'loving' terms—before she can find the energy for 'some new kind of start'. As a result, the mode of these plays wavers between the tragic, the satiric, and the *engagé*, and represents a furtherance of familiar Irish tragicomic kinds into quite unfamiliar tones and territories. In this way *Bailegangaire* becomes the name for a radical new figuring, a re-representation, of the Irish rural, or of what *Conversations on a Homecoming* calls 'the country-and-western system itself', and for an engagement with inherited theatrical and literary forms which is both appreciative and critical. Tom Murphy's theatre too has a deep understanding of the need for 'some new kind of start'.

5. *Coda: Land Erosion*

This chapter began with an account of some of the ways in which Eamon de Valera's glossing of the rural Irish world, and in which that gloss formed part of the propaganda of his Fianna Fail party in Ireland between the 1930s and the 1950s, acted as challenge and goad for a number of Irish writers. In Colm Toibin's novel *The Heather Blazing* (1992), the central character, a Dublin High Court judge, Eamon Redmond, has been named after de Valera, who figures briefly as a character in the book. Redmond comes from a strongly Republican family: his grandfather fought in 1916; his father played an always-unspecified, never-discussed part in the War of Independence

and the Civil War; and Eamon himself as an adolescent boy has
made a rousing speech at a Fianna Fail election campaign, where
he is noticed by Seán Lemass, the future Irish prime minister. As
a judge, much of his work has come as a state prosecutor on
behalf of the Fianna Fail government. The book's title derives
from a Republican song, 'Boolavogue', a great rabble-rouser set
during the rebellion of 1798.

The novel is, therefore, on one level, an account of the fate of
the Republican or nationalist ideal in contemporary Southern
Irish society, as Toibin perceives it: the judgements we witness Eamon Redmond making, which greatly distress the rest
of his family, are part of the deeply conservative, Catholic,
misogynistic apparatus of the Irish state. But the intricate structure of this superficially very quiet and understated novel inter-
weaves Eamon's present with his vulnerable, unmothered,
lonely childhood; the book oscillates between present and past,
experience and memory. The result is both a sympathetically
engaged *Bildungsroman* and a novel of retrospect in late middle
age; and the combination forms a compelling depiction of the
forces which tie the individual to his historical moment in post-
revolutionary Ireland. The book's structure also binds the rural
east of Ireland of Eamon's childhood and present summer vaca-
tions—which contains such luminous nationalist locations as the
Vinegar Hill (Boolavogue) of the failed rebellion of 1798—to
the metropolitan Dublin of his present power relations and social existence. The subtly generous but sceptical register of
Eamon's state of being, which reveals him as a man of probity
who is nevertheless conscious of his lack of both theological and
political belief, testifies to Toibin's measured and temperate, but
still-vigilant portrayal of a society some of whose most cherished
ideals are now in a state of terminal collapse. The collapse is
insistently pointed by the fact that Eamon's holiday home stands
on land being eroded by the sea. The consolations of a
martyrological Republican history, and of an assuaging Irish
marine landscape, are both, presumably, included in what this
trope places under potential erasure, writing a culture in terms
of a topography:

It had been so gradual, this erosion, a matter of time, lumps of clay, small boulders studded with stones becoming loose and falling away, the sea gnawing at the land. It was all so strange, year after year, the slow disappearance of one contour to be replaced by another, it was hard to notice that anything had happened until something substantial . . . fell down on to the strand.[21]

4

Views of Dublin

An eighteenth century prospect to the sea—
River haze; gulls; spires glitter in the distance
Above faint multitudes. Barely audible
A murmur of soft, wicked laughter rises.
Dublin, the umpteenth city of confusion...

A theatre for the quick articulate,
The agonized genteel, their artful watchers...
Malice as entertainment. Asinine feast
Of sowthistles and brambles! And there dead men,
Half hindered by dead men, tear down dead beauty.

(Thomas Kinsella, 'Phoenix Park' (1968))[1]

1. Troubles

Talking to his friend Frank Budgen, James Joyce once famously remarked that his aim in *Ulysses* was to 'give a picture of Dublin so complete that if the city one day suddenly disappeared from the earth it could be reconstructed out of my book'.[2] In many ways the city of Dublin as it was in Joyce's day has in fact disappeared from the earth, victim of heavy urban development and reconstruction since the 1960s; but the encyclopaedic comprehensiveness of Joyce's depiction of it in his novel has acted as both goad and inhibition to many subsequent writers. The shadow of *Ulysses* falls with varying degrees of heaviness over numerous later literary treatments of the city; and Joyce is, as we shall see, a point of reference in many of these texts.

The Dublin re-created in Joyce is not merely topographical: it is also historical and political. Towards the end of the book's 'Circe' episode, in which its characters and the very narrative and texture of the writing itself undergo nightmarish transfor-

mation, the city goes up in apocalyptic flames, destroyed in
various kinds of battle, including a partly absurd listing of
Irish historical encounters ('Wolfe Tone against Henry Grattan, Smith O'Brien against Daniel O'Connell, Michael Davitt
against Isaac Butt', and so on). This is, at least in part, Joyce's
incorporation into *Ulysses*—set in 1904 but not published until
1922, and therefore very much a historical novel—of material
drawn from, or dependent on, the Easter Rising of 1916, when
members of the Irish Republican Brotherhood, led by the poet
Padraig Pearse, engaged in a determined but hopeless military
operation, proclaiming an Irish Republic. Easily captured after
bloody street-fighting in central Dublin, the fifteen leaders of the
rebellion were court-martialled and summarily executed, and
became subsequently the focus of a republican martyrology.
Joyce's attitudes to Irish nationalism, and to the colonial mentality which produced it, are themselves on display at various
places in *Ulysses*, crucially in the 'Cyclops' episode, where the
Jewish Leopold Bloom has to endure and combat anti-Semitic
persecution. The nationalist rhetoric of this episode is, in places,
continuous with Pearse's appeal to romantic or even quasi-
mystical conceptions of nationality, race, and blood and with the
anti-Semitism of Arthur Griffiths, founder of Sinn Fein; and the
Citizen's citation of 'the memory of the dead' as an inspiration to
present action is deeply embedded in those traditions of Irish
nationalism and Republicanism which had their flowering in the
Easter Rising.[3]

If Joyce's attitudes to the Rising are present but obliquely
rendered in the historicity of *Ulysses*, Yeats is famously more
direct in his responses, and subsequently to the War of Independence and the Civil War also. In his volumes *Michael
Robartes and the Dancer* (1921) and *The Tower* (1928) he brings
the period into writing with immense authority in some of his
greatest poems. Easter 1916, indeed, is named, following the
earlier 'September 1913', as if it is to be given its ultimate definition in the very title of the poem 'Easter 1916', where Yeats
meditates on the historical moment which, in his view, transforms idiosyncratic and routine individualism into common

revolutionary purpose, but only at extreme personal cost: the
poem produces from its meditation the intensely memorable
and frequently cited oxymoronic aphorism 'A terrible beauty is
born'. In the same volume, *Michael Robartes and the Dancer*,
Yeats writes, in 'Sixteen Dead Men', a poem that understands
very early (it was written in 1916 or 1917) the martyrology that
will be constructed out of the execution of the leaders of the
Rising. It projects, accurately, the violent Irish future at nurture
in what will become the ideologically loaded legend of 'those
dead men . . . loitering there | To stir the boiling pot'. In *The
Tower* the magnificent sequence 'Meditations in Time of Civil
War' pits the urgency of Yeats's symbolizing and myth-making
desire—his need to discover 'befitting emblems of adversity'—
against a baffled and hopeless register of the actuality of civil
strife. The poet-sage in his tower, constructing his magical and
mythological systems, is buffeted out of self-entrancement when
'they trundled down the road | That dead young soldier in his
blood'. In these oppositions between imaginative capacity and
historical actuality Yeats's most intimately apprehended poetic
is placed under challenging self-exposure, becoming vulnerable
where it would be dominant; and the result is the deep embitterment which figures again in 'Nineteen Hundred and Nineteen',
his poem on the War of Independence in *The Tower*, with its
definitive stanza:

> Now days are dragon-ridden, the nightmare
> Rides upon sleep: a drunken soldiery
> Can leave the mother, murdered at her door,
> To crawl in her own blood, and go scot-free;
> The night can sweat with terror as before
> We pieced our thoughts into philosophy,
> And planned to bring the world under a rule,
> Who are but weasels fighting in a hole.

In Yeats, and to some extent in Joyce, then, the matter which
has continued to perturb the work of a number of later writers
achieves notable, permanent, and unignorable expressions.
When the Rising of 1916 and the Troubles of the 1920s figure
again in Irish writing, they do so in ways inevitably referential to

these initial treatments of them. In this chapter I want to begin with an account of some of the writing after Yeats and Joyce in which that revolutionary crisis is represented: the contemporaneous plays of Sean O'Casey; the subsequent return to the moment and its aftermath in the work of Brendan Behan; and Francis Stuart's incorporation of it in his autobiographical novel *Black List, Section H*.

The most notable extended representation of the Dublin of the period of Easter 1916, the War of Independence, and the Civil War is offered in the first three plays of Sean O'Casey: *The Shadow of a Gunman* (1925), set during the War of Independence in 1920, *Juno and the Paycock* (1925), set during the Civil War in 1922, and *The Plough and the Stars* (1926), set in November 1915 and Easter Week 1916. All three plays have as their location Dublin's appalling tenement housing, which was then the worst in Europe, and their characters are the socially deprived and depressed working classes who occupy the tenements, the people whom one of the stage directions in *The Shadow of a Gunman* calls 'the cave-dwellers of Dublin'. Some of O'Casey's elaborate, novelistic stage directions emphasize the way these tenements were ironically once the most fashionable Georgian residences in the city; and their dilapidation and disintegration act as a visual stage correlative of the various dilapidations and disintegrations of the lives of the plays' characters.[4]

The tenements are, first, frail and flimsy dwellings—'rookeries', they are called in *The Shadow of a Gunman*—where curtains substitute for doors, where what doors there are don't shut, and where, as a result, the lives of individuals and families are constantly interrupted by the intrusion of others. The permanent coming and going on stage is an emblem of the rootless lives of the tenants themselves, as the circumstances of joblessness, marital distress, and civil unrest make them all to some degree transients. In addition, the lack of privacy produces their characteristic form of discourse—a vituperative invective, all animosity, resentment, and envy—which often threatens to disintegrate into physical violence. The vituperation is expressed in that extremely accurate Dublinese which O'Casey's early work is famous for managing to represent orthographically. His insider knowledge of this place and this language makes of all three plays strongly engaged pieces of socialist analysis. Their critique of Irish nationalism is embedded in, and bolstered by the hard-won knowledge expressed most forcefully by the character known as 'The Covey' in *The Plough and the Stars*: 'There's only one war worth havin': th' war for th' economic emancipation of th' proletariat.'

The Covey is, however, loud-mouthed, self-opinionated, and vulgarly brash. Elsewhere too, where we might expect sympathetic characterization to accompany ideological correctness, O'Casey decisively defeats expectation. In *The Shadow of a Gunman* the poet and Shelleyan Davoren ends as a self-confessed 'poltroon' after setting in motion the circumstances in which the girl who loves him, Minnie Powell, is shot by the Black and Tans; and in *Juno and the Paycock* the union organizer Charles Bentham abandons his girlfriend Mary Boyle when she becomes pregnant, and flees to England. O'Casey's critics have often discovered in these characterizations both a nihilistic despair about all politics, whether socialist or nationalist, and a stereotyping of all men as feckless, cowardly, and incompetent, and of all women as incarnating qualities of resolute humanitarian fortitude and endurance—with the consequence that the plays become sentimental or melodramatic, or both.

The basic patterns of O'Casey's work are clearly comprehended by this critique. In *Juno and the Paycock* the wife and mother Juno is the capable provider, whereas her husband Jack Boyle is the work-shy and alcoholic Paycock; in *The Plough and the Stars* Bessie Burgess, the 'Orange' imperial sympathizer, and apparent target of the play's satirical mockery for much of its course, becomes the heroically dignified defender of the victim Nora Clitheroe during her descent into insanity following a miscarriage. Nora's husband Jack, on the other hand, is killed in the Easter Rising, in which he has fought not out of principled Republican belief but out of the schoolboy heroics which instil in him the cowardly shame of disengagement. Even if the pattern is briefly unstitched—when Bessie dies, shockingly blaming Nora as a 'bitch' responsible for the incident in which she has been shot, for instance—it does seem the fundamental programme of O'Casey's imagination.

As such, it may be read as the inevitable consequence of his deep early disenchantment with Irish politics. He had joined the Gaelic League and learnt Irish, had been a member of the Irish Republican Brotherhood, had worked with the socialist James Larkin during the Dublin lock-out of 1913, and had acted as secretary of the Irish Citizen Army, a post he resigned when it joined forces with the Irish Volunteers, who were hostile to unionization, in order to fight in 1916. The concept of an armed struggle against British rule was one he came to find increasingly distasteful. In *The Plough and the Stars*, whose title evokes the pattern of the flag of the Citizen Army, some of the most famous speeches of Padraig Pearse on the necessity for blood sacrifice ('Bloodshed is a cleansing and a sanctifying thing') are plundered and placed in radically undermining satirical contexts. Seamus Deane has observed that, strange as it may seem to think of this socialist, Republican, and later Stalinist communist as a pacifist, this is the ultimate conclusion to be drawn from the work.[5]

If the politics of the plays are confused, however, and indeterminate, and if some of O'Casey's later political alignments seem insupportable, this is perhaps the result of a larger form of transience or traditionlessness in his writing. Born into the Dublin Protestant working class and an autodidact, O'Casey probably had a certain social and cultural isolation virtually plotted into his system. The politics of the plays give the impression of having been worked out in embittered effortfulness from the flimsiest of foundations: so that the appeal to an apolitical realm of womanly 'humanity' must have been almost a psychic inevitability for this writer, however hopelessly romantic such an option appears in the context of the *realpolitik* which his plays otherwise reveal as actually conditioning peoples' lives during this revolutionary period. The isolation finds its reflection too in the actual forms and structures of his theatre, where there is what sometimes seems a chaos, or a 'chassis'—as Jack Boyle famously calls it—of representational modes, in which the basic realism of the genre opens up or fractures into the heavy use of literary and Biblical quotation; an almost stylized or quasi-expressionist, gestural figuring of antagonism and opposition; a great deal of Irish historical and mythological reference; and a prominent use of music and song—love-song, hymn, popular and political balladry—which closely associates his drama with the popular culture of the music-hall and with certain Brechtian forms of alienation and affront. The plays, that is to say, convey the strong sense of a dramatist making it up as he goes along, beginning with no sense of an integral theatrical tradition, but inventing one for himself from the orts and fragments lying to hand while he is actually engaged in the creative act. If such a lack of sustenance was eventually responsible for his falling victim to over-ambitious structures and various kinds of over-writing in his later work, it produces in these three plays an inspired resourcefulness in which an energy of indignation more than meets its match in a new energy of the language itself, and in an assured richness of characterization.

In Brendan Behan's work there is a comparable sense that dramatic structures are being newly forged as the result of urgent emotional need, and they are drawn partly, again, from music-hall tradition and also now partly from O'Casey himself. The use of music and song is taken to revue-like lengths in *The Hostage* (1958), which was shaped largely by its production in English in Joan Littlewood's Theatre Workshop in Stratford East, after it had been originally written and performed in Irish as *An Giall* in the same year. In *The Hostage* and in the earlier *The Quare Fellow* (1954) the structural raggedness and intense musicality are both productive of enormous, sometimes chaotic vitality. This amounts virtually to a principle of ironic form, since the plots of both prominently include death, in the shape of judicial murder. *The Quare Fellow* is set in Mountjoy Prison in Dublin on the day of the execution of a murderer, and the play painfully and sometimes hideously exposes the brutalities of its occasion, as both warders and prisoners, in preparing for the execution, reveal the shame, terror, and guilt in which the realities of judicial murder mutually entrap them. *The Hostage*, a more complex—if to some critics a less satisfactory—play, is set in a Dublin lodging-house-cum-brothel owned by an ex-IRA soldier, the English, public-school-educated Monsewer. Since Monsewer is in something approaching his dotage, however, the house is actually managed by another old IRA man, Pat; and both he and Monsewer have fought in 1916 and in the War of Independence and, as Republicans, in the Civil War.

On the night on which the play is set the house is being used as a safe house for a couple of contemporary IRA men and the very young kidnapped British soldier, Leslie Williams, who is being held as 'hostage' for an equally young IRA man due to be executed the following morning in Belfast Jail. During the play's lengthy course the house's extraordinary occupants—prostitutes, homosexuals, IRA men, religious maniacs, Russian soldiers—are swept up into an increasingly manic dramatic action which culminates in quite unconvincing last-minute revelations of secret identities, police spies, and an armed attack during which the soldier is killed. Despite the ludicrous ending, the play's action has great strength as itself a kind of dance of, or against, death. In particular, the mania of unrestrainedly promiscuous sexuality is in fact a gravely poignant counterpoint to what is Behan's recurrent anxiety and distress: the terrible reality of young male bodies about to be dead, subject to the violence of either judicial murder or organizational reprisal.

At one point in *The Hostage* Behan incorporates a piece of self-reflexive self-rebuke, when he is himself named as the author of a song just sung:

SOLDIER: Brendan Behan, he's too anti-British.
OFFICER: Too anti-Irish, you mean. Bejasus, wait till we get him back home. We'll give him what-for for making fun of the Movement.
SOLDIER [*to audience*]: He doesn't mind coming over here and taking your money.
PAT: He'd sell his country for a pint.

This bravely expresses and compresses that entanglement of affinities, anxieties, and disengagements in Behan's political and artistic career. He is the once-jailed, insider Republican now exposing the outmoded fanaticism and philistinism of the contemporary IRA ('the Movement'), regarding it as frozen into absurdly heroic postures and serenely indifferent to any actual 'social question', having exchanged an early consorting with socialism for a hardened Catholic reaction. He is nevertheless also the former Republican who still insists on exposing again (and for an English audience) the enormities of British behaviour in Dublin during 1916 and the War of Independence, when soldiers shelled civilians in their tenement houses. He is the inhabitant of the Free State and the Republic disgusted that its penal codes are continuous with those of the overthrown British state ('the Free State didn't change anything more than the badge on the warders' caps', says Dunlavin in *The Quare Fellow*). He is the Irish writer making a buck out of an English audience, and possibly, as a result, playing up to their sense of what an 'Irish' writer might be like—their assumption, for instance, that he will write in, or at least have the decency to translate himself into the English language; or, worse, that he will be a stereotypical Irish alcoholic, the personality construction 'Brendan Behan', famously and garrulously drunk on British television, selling his country for the pint that was all too soon to kill him.

In *The Hostage* this troubled, contumacious sensibility could be said to account for itself by uncovering the political and cultural network of British colonialism in Ireland in which it was structured, which prominently includes the after-effects of British withdrawal which left the six counties of Northern Ireland as a future battleground. The play's almost phantasmagoric characterizations and plotting witness to Behan's arguing out with himself the reality of the politics which formed him. Just as O'Casey ultimately figures a release from politics itself as the truly desirable, if utopian, state, Behan's exhaustion shapes itself in *The Hostage* into a dream of alternative sexuality when he charts the hesitant but developing relationship between the captured British soldier and the Irish 'skivvy' and country-girl Teresa. Leslie, the national serviceman under duress, is almost totally innocent of Irish politics or history; and both he and

Teresa are orphans. When they tell each other their lonely, abandoned childhood stories, in Englishes which are so varied as to be at points mutually unintelligible, and when the Irish Catholic Teresa gives the uncomprehendingly British Protestant Leslie a present of her 'miraculous medal' (an image of the Virgin Mary worn around the neck), Behan offers an emblem of release from the entrapping stereotypes which is as quick and tender as that other such relationship in later Irish drama, between the English soldier Yolland and the Irish woman Maire in Brian Friel's *Translations* (which may well be indebted to it). If that alternative exists in the realm of sexuality, however (and coexists there with the play's inclusion and defence of homosexuality), the fact that the possibility is very fragile is itself of course finally figured in the brevity of the relationship: Leslie leaves Teresa's bed almost immediately to be killed. Although love and the promise of permanent remembrance precede the bitterness of Leslie's posthumous song, Brendan Behan's imagination is anchored in the soldier's death more confidently than it is anywhere else:

> The bells of hell
> Go ting-a-ling-a-ling,
> For you but not for me,
> Oh death, where is thy sting-a-ling-a-ling?
> Or grave thy victory?

The fact that Behan was capable of the composite ironies and horrors inherent in the use, in such a context, of this well-known song of the First World War should have protected him from the condescension he frequently received while alive and continues sometimes to receive, when he is not simply neglected, in contemporary criticism and theatre.

The experiences of 1916 and the 1920s have unsurprisingly remained the focus of other historical fictionalizing in Irish writing, some of it subsequent to Behan: in, for instance, the very uneven novels of Liam O'Flaherty, *The Assassin* (1928) and the much longer-meditated *The Informer* (1950); in Julia O'Faolain's *No Country for Young Men* (1980); in, as we have seen, many novels of the Big House; and in Tom Murphy's 'documentary drama' *The Patriot Game* (1991). They also figure prominently in one of the strangest novels to have come out of modern Ireland, Francis Stuart's autobiographical *Black List, Section H* (published in 1971, but written in 1961–2). Stuart fought on the Republican side during the Civil War, and that experience is written centrally into this novel, along with his subsequent highly controversial time in Germany during the Second World War.

Black List, Section H disguises its author as the eponymous 'H' but refers to others under their actual names. These include, notably, H's wife Iseult Gonne, to whom Yeats once proposed, and who had had an affair with Ezra Pound; Iseult's mother, Maud, the constant object of Yeats's desire and the subject of some of his finest poems, with whom H has an extremely fraught relationship; and William Butler Yeats himself, the poet as an Irish senator and Nobel Prize winner towards the end of the period of the Literary Revival. H is born of Ulster Unionist stock in Australia, where his father has died mysteriously in H's childhood (by suicide, it is strongly hinted). He subsequently endures an excruciatingly difficult marriage with Iseult in and outside Dublin, is encouraged and praised as a writer by Yeats, fights and is imprisoned during the Civil War, and spends much time in 1920s and 1930s bohemian London strenuously learning (successfully) how to overcome deep sexual inhibition and incompetence. Then, at the outbreak of war, he quite unpredictably takes up a university post in Hitler's Germany, where he stays for the duration, occasionally making broadcasts on behalf of the Nazis. Throughout all of this H writes and publishes novels (Stuart has himself published twenty-two) and anguishes over the role of the writer in modern civilization, rejecting, even while admiring, many of the most notable examples (Joyce, Céline, Lawrence).

In addition to being an acerbically un-illusioned but still-buoyant account of the Dublin—and the London—of its time, *Black List, Section H* constitutes an apologia of a kind for the scandalous political alignments of its hero's life. Neither his attachment to the Republican cause in the Civil War nor his willingness to act on behalf of the Nazis during the Second World War is ascribable to the usual political motivations. The book is, rather, a study of abjection in which H's often expressed theory, and certainly his practice, of writing are offered as a counter to what he regards as almost all the unavailing assumptions of the modern world. With a sometimes queasily uncertain combination of arrogance and vulnerability, H acknowledges the fact that his writing derives from a profound neurosis, into which he wills himself further for the sake of the work: 'The only side to take was the one considered most unpardonable by the circle in which he found himself . . . Better the infected sovereign psyche than one that shared in a general righteousness that didn't belong to it.'

Readers may well interpret this infection as the result of the death of the father during H's childhood (as neuroses have been judged to have originated in the cases of such other writers as Coleridge, Cowper, Berryman, and Plath), although H himself never explicitly does this. As an apology for the disaster of H's political decisions, however, it may seem a dangerous kind of special pleading; and the book does make for extremely perturbing reading, as H follows a logic of extremity. Stuart's writing itself—tremulous and sometimes, it appears, almost randomly organized, but nevertheless driven by an urgency which catches the reader up into its own excess—is the utterance of a corrosively unregulated, permanently restless sensibility.[6]

There is little question, however—particularly since H himself raises the question ('He couldn't be certain he hadn't been infected by the plague')—of the paradoxical and obsessive purity of motive at the ground of the decision. We actually believe him when H says that he hopes for the defeat of Germany, even as he broadcasts to Ireland on its behalf; and we are both appalled and compelled by the rationale of identification with the fate of the Jews: 'he had to experience, in his own probably small degree, some of what they suffered, and, on one level, even more, because he could not claim their innocence.' This may be read as a fanatical refusal of artistic complicity in conventional social mores; as a psychotic fetishizing of victimization and 'dishonour'; or as, of course, a piece of self-deluding retrospective rationalization. The reader's uncertainty makes for the lack of any easy accommodation with this long, in many ways monstrous Irish journey to the end of the night where, at the close, H, incarcerated alone in a cell, waits for an utterly uncertain future: 'Whatever it was that was at the other end there was no way of telling. It might be a howl of final despair or the profound silence might be broken by certain words that he didn't yet know how to listen for.'

2. *Disappointments, Differences*

The poetry of Austin Clarke everywhere makes reference to Dublin's topography in a way that draws, as Hugh Maxton has observed, on traditions of both Gaelic and eighteenth-century English loco-descriptive verse.[7] The streets of Dublin, its public buildings and parks, and its environs are named again and again in the poems, which form a sort of imaginative gazetteer of the capital. If the reiterated names are an index of Clarke's intimacy with the city in which he spent most of his life, however, they are also the localization of a long, bitter, satirical engagement with its polity and governance. His spikily socialist poetry of rebuke, working its way out of any vestige of a Yeatsian rhetorical magnificence, is fuelled in particular by an anticlericalism deeply resentful of the collusion between Church and state in the Ireland of the mid-century: in notable poems such as 'Penal Law', 'Unmarried Mothers', and 'Three Poems about Children' he scornfully derides the social abuses consequent on the collusion. The disgust, which combines Swiftian excoriation with vulnerable desolation, also sustains a poetry of appalled empathy in such vignettes as 'Martha Blake at Fifty-One', in which a devout Dublin Catholic spinster dies a hideous death unattended by any priest of the Church to which she has been scrupulously faithful:

> Unpitied, wasting with diarrhoea
> And the constant strain,

> Poor Child of Mary with one idea,
>   She ruptured a small vein,
> Bled inwardly to jazz. No priest
>   Came. She had been anointed
> Two days before, yet knew no peace:
>   Her last breath, disappointed.

The queasy physical repellence of that, and its evocation of a metaphysical disappointment, are entirely characteristic of Clarke, whose poetic finds a viscerally acute form for its distresses.

This is crucially the case in one of his finest works, the long poem *Mnemosyne Lay in Dust* (1966). Taking as its subject Clarke's own experience of mental breakdown in 1919, and his incarceration in St Patrick's Hospital—the asylum bequeathed to Dublin by Jonathan Swift—it partly fictionalizes its occasion by creating the representative autobiographical figure of 'Maurice Devane', and it also richly extends its reading of psychological disintegration with a parallel or intertwined reading of Irish political history. A poem obviously meditated—and morosely meditated—for an exceptionally long time, given the almost fifty-year gap between its publication and the time of the experiences it recounts, *Mnemosyne Lay in Dust* both chillingly exposes the routinely dreadful medical and psychiatric practices of the Dublin hospitals of 1919 and also situates them as part of a political history of rebellion against colonial power.[8] In a poem which, in its fragmented, elliptical narrative, tensely reconstructs sensations of paranoia, derangement, and disorientation—to all of which kinds of 'unselfing' the specificities of named Dublin locations form an ironically stable foil—Devane suffers many hallucinatory delusions. The most powerful of these is his conception of himself as a Republican gunman in Co. Limerick during the War of Independence, which was actually being fought during Clarke's/Devane's incarceration. Devane's illness also results in a refusal to eat; and in this he regards himself as at one with the hunger-strikers of Irish Republican history, where the potentially suicidal rejection of food becomes the only possible, and ultimate, protest of the powerless against British rule

(Maxton notes, for instance, that the Lord Mayor of Cork, Terence MacSwiney, who endured one of the most famous of Irish hunger-strikes, died on 20 October 1920, shortly after the terrifying experience of Devane himself in the poem).[9]

The sexual neurosis frequently hinted at as the source of Devane's disintegration is therefore intermeshed with the political circumstances through which he has lived; and the tenth section of the poem, which evokes soldiers around a campfire with 'a history-book lying on the floor', is explicit about the analogy being made between a sexual and a political distress:

> They lie, in the dark,
> Watching the fire, on the edge
> Of a storybook jungle: they watch
> The high boots of the colonists.

This is oblique; but one way of reading it is to register the force of the way 'they'—that is, the inhabitants of a Dublin lunatic asylum in 1919—imagine themselves as soldiers terrorized by an occupying, colonial power. In that imagining, they offer a political understanding of their own plight: which is, that to be dominated by such forces, and to suffer the consequences of the oppositional subversion and terrorism to which they inevitably give rise, is itself a kind of socio-cultural insanity. In proposing such an interpretation of the relation between the psycho-sexual and the political, *Mnemosyne Lay in Dust* writes a Dublin of the individual human body and mind: it identifies a private nightmare as a catastrophic public history. In this way it gives a new resonance to Stephen Dedalus's sense of history as 'a nightmare from which I am trying to awake'.[10]

Thomas Kinsella has edited Clarke and, in his own poem 'Magnanimity', he celebrates the elder poet's seventieth birthday. Kinsella shares with Clarke both a Dublin poetic topography—many of his poems are titled with Dublin place-names: 'Baggot Street Deserta', 'Westland Row', 'Phoenix Park', 'Ely Place', '38 Phoenix Street', and so on—and a dejection at the failure of the revolutionary idealism which inspired the War of Independence. In the sequence 'Nightwalker' (1968) he offers a scathing rebuke to political opportunism and cynicism, which is figured as a bestiary in which fox and weasel fight—a trope drawing, presumably, on the 'weasels fighting in a hole' in Yeats's 'Nineteen Hundred and Nineteen':

> Among us, behind locked doors, the ministers
> Are working, with a sureness of touch found early
> In the nation's birth—the blood of enemies
> And brothers dried on their hide long ago.

Small wonder, given such disgust, that one of the poems in the sequence concludes: 'I think this is the Sea of Disappointment', which makes an allegory from the word Clarke uses literally at the close of 'Martha Blake at Fifty-One'. 'Nightwalker' also includes, however, an invocation to Joyce—'Watcher in the tower, be with me now'—and an evocation of him as both 'father of authors' and 'foxhunter' (although this latter is peculiarly crossed with an image of the young, in Kinsella's view ruthlessly opportunistic politician Charles Haughey, later to become Taoiseach). For a poet whose work often attends so intimately to the details and textures of Dublin's political life, the Joycean models of satirical exposure, of dispassionate scrutiny and critique, are deeply formative; and they continue to influence, in different ways, the sequences which follow 'Nightwalker' in Kinsella's developing and increasingly complex work.

In the early 'Baggot Street Deserta', one of his best-known poems, published in *Another September* (1958), he imagines the heads of dreamers lying 'mesmerised in Dublin's beds | Flashing with images, Adam's morse'. Initiated by 'Phoenix Park' (1968) and published in sections or sequences from his own Peppercanister Press in Dublin, Kinsella's 'Peppercanister Poems' may be regarded as the transcriptions of some of these dreams and the tapping out of a very intricate morse. These austere, often exacerbated and self-exacerbated poems explore dream and nightmare landscapes, inquire into the sources of sexuality and creativity, and acutely probe psychological distress in ways that constitute a phantasmagoric autobiography. Nevertheless, many of the poems also continue to be rooted in, and named for, specific Dublin places; and, like Clarke in *Mnemosyne Lay in Dust*, Kinsella traces the psycho-biography along the lines of Irish social and political history as well as those of family origin and attachment. Two of the finest sequences, 'The Messenger' and 'St. Catherine's Clock', which are both collected in *Blood and Family* (1988), give these tracings some of their most lucid shapes. The former, which shares its title with that of a now-defunct Irish Catholic devotional magazine, inquires into paternity and sexuality, Kinsella going constantly 'deeper'—as deep as into the grave—to explore his relationship with his father. The title also derives, however, from his father's boyhood job as a Post Office messenger; and in a moment which has the vivid immediacy and etched memorability of a Joycean epiphany, Kinsella figures his father, in this role, as that other kind of messenger, the classical god Mercury:

> He unprops the great Post Office bicycle
> from the sewing machine and wheels it through the passage
> by odours of apron and cabbage-water and whitewashed damp
>
> through the shop and into the street.
> It faces uphill. The urchin mounts. I see
> a flash of pedals! And a clean pair of heels!

In later life Kinsella senior had been a worker in Guinness's brewery in Thomas Street and one of the first members of an organized union there. 'The Messenger' therefore also intertwines the father's socialist politics with its biographical or 'genetic' material, composing a rich act of filial piety. In 'St. Catherine's Clock' Thomas Street figures once more as the location of autobiography, but the fragments of reminiscence of working-class Dublin are now dated '1938', and they are juxtaposed with vignettes dated 1803 (when the nationalist hero Robert Emmet was executed on a gallows in front of St Catherine's Church), 1792, and 1740. These serve to offer Kinsella's developing identity as palimpsestic with significant moments of Dublin's own identity as a colonial capital. The 1803 fragment, for instance, is a reflection on an engraving by George Cruickshank commemorating the murder of a Lord Kilwarden by a 'pack of hatted simians'—by, that is, people caricatured in a way entirely typical of English representations of the Irish in the nineteenth century. Kinsella's is only exceptionally the kind of poetry to parade its politics in any obvious way; but 'St. Catherine's Clock' is nevertheless manifestly a political poem which puts on display the articulate intellectual subjectivity of a poet whose forebears are regarded as 'simian' by the English caricaturist. In the ongoing sequences of these Peppercanister poems the city of Dublin—referred to in the title of one of the sequences as 'Centre City'—is given one of its most unpredictable and experimental modern representations.

Eavan Boland, writing about the impact of Kinsella's *Downstream* when it was published in 1962, observes that 'To a tradition only beginning to realize that Irish identity was a matter of fragments, it brought a music which dignified fragmentation and honoured doubt'.[11] Her own poetry reads the fragmentation of its tradition from the perspective of an Irish woman poet—giving both of those adjectives emphasis and close scrutiny—and offers, partly in its imagery and tropes of suburban Dublin, a radical but undoctrinaire feminist interruption to the traditionally masculine course, and discourse, of Irish poetry. The self-conscious deliberation with which this has been pursued as a developing method and programme in her work is made clear in her book of autobiographical-cum-critical writings, *Object Lessons* (1995). Here she explores her sense of what a woman's poetry might be in contemporary Ireland by focusing on two key stages of her own evolution: her education at Trinity College and her life as a wife, mother, and poet in the suburb of Dundrum, under the Dublin mountains. The atmospheres of both urban and suburban Dublin intertwine themselves with her critique in this tentative and subtle—if occasionally rather self-aggrandizing—book, where recovered autobiographical detail consorts with her inquiry into the concepts of 'woman' and 'nation' in an Irish woman poet's life and writing.

The inquiry focuses on particular womanly silences in Irish history, read as emblematic of powerlessness. These prominently include that of her own grandmother and that of an imagined woman inhabitant of the workhouse run by her great-grandfather. Boland desires not that her poetry should take any usual form of feminist separatism but rather that it should embody this powerlessness as itself a subversive agent, revising male metaphors of poetic empowerment. In this attempt the example of Sylvia Plath is, not surprisingly, crucial; but Patrick Kavanagh, in his Dublin poems, is also arrestingly offered as 'an example of dissidence . . . of someone who had used the occasion of his life to rebuff the expectations and preconceptions of the Irish poem'.[12] The combination of Plath and Kavanagh as mentors is a clear indication of the double heritage which Boland aims to hand on in work which might constitute 'a magnetic field where the created [that is, the woman] returns as the creator'.[13]

The poems themselves are frequently self-conscious about their revisionist nature. The titles of individual volumes—such as her first book, *New Territory* (1967), and *Outside History* (1990)—evoke those concepts of both possibility and marginality which the poems constantly circle and insinuate; and the titles of some of the poems themselves court a deliberate and disarming bathos: 'Ode to Suburbia', 'Suburban Woman', 'Domestic Interior', and so on. A typical method is to set her suburban existence, with its ordinary interiors and exteriors, its landscapes of kitchen and garden, its equipment of kettle, washing-machine, and lawn-mower, and its routines of child-collecting, nappy-washing, and ironing, against a sense of historical absence and silence and against an awareness of the violence and dislocation which this quiet, domesticated space keeps at bay. In 'The War Horse', for instance, from her volume of that title published in 1975, the suburban garden is invaded by a horse—probably that of travellers (gypsies) who once camped on the land which became the suburb—whose atavistic memory of his earlier place becomes an emblem of a repressed history of 'burned countryside, illicit braid: | A cause ruined before, a world betrayed.'

The Dublin suburb, the place of the woman and of the 'lethal | rapine of routine', thus gets into Irish poetry in a memorable way; but it is also used as the basis for various kinds of satire, as when Boland offers a swingeing 'Tirade for the Mimic Muse', that woman created in the image of men, in the pivotal volume *In her Own Image* (1980), and as the location of historical scrutiny and poetic transformation. In 'The Journey', for instance, the title poem of a book of 1986, she cites the sixth book of Virgil's *Aeneid*, with its dead infants at the entrance to Hades. Observing that there are no poems in praise of the antibiotic (which has, of course, saved countless later children from infant death, and therefore saved mothers from misery), she opens the poem up into a dream-vision journey through the underworld, in which the poet is accompanied by Sappho, as Dante had been accompanied by Virgil himself in the *Commedia*. The final depiction of Sappho's poetic laying-on of hands, which offers the spectacle of a womanly 'tradition' in the act of self-construction, may be read as a counterpart, and a counter, to Seamus Heaney's Dantean poem 'Station Island' of 1984, in which all his visionary encounters are with male poets and mentors.

The command and assurance of this poem are matched by the mordant wit of 'Mise Eire' in the same book, whose title, meaning 'I am Ireland', alludes to both a famous poem by Padraig Pearse and to the immensely popular piece of music which Seán O'Riada composed in 1966 as a celebration of the fiftieth anniversary of the 1916 Rising. Turning some inheritances from a male nationalist tradition on their heads, Boland here uncovers certain images of women silenced in Irish history, and offers an adversarial and combative role as self-definition, proposing the marginalized woman—in this case a prostitute—as an emblem of defiance and endurance. It is a prime instance in her work of how, in the title of one of the pieces in *Object Lessons*, women's poems go about the business of 'making the difference':

> I am the woman—
> a sloven's mix
> of silk at the wrists,
> a sort of dove-strut
> in the precincts of the garrison.[14]

Paul Durcan's poetry is in some senses continuous with the effort being made in Boland's: it writes a subversively satirical account of contemporary Irish social, political, and ecclesiastical life which frequently concentrates on the treatment of women and includes the several masculine vulnerabilities of homo-erotic desire, mental breakdown, and traumatic divorce. It also—exceptionally for a writer from the Republic—offers a view of the North which flies in the face of all nationalist senti-ment with a critique of the IRA and its apologists; although Durcan's critics might well maintain that the critique depends, perhaps presumptuously, on his being, precisely, a long way from the Troubles themselves, as both southern and middle-class. The poetry makes its own obeisance to Patrick Kavanagh, in the poem 'November 1967' (the date of Kavanagh's death), celebrating his demotic address and satirically democratic spirit. But it also sails off into an often surreal, anecdotal, apparently near-improvisatory poetic in which contemporary Irish experi-ence is refracted through a prism of absurdity in a way at once nonchalant and venomous. The seemingly spontaneous quality of some of these poems has the drawback that technique is sometimes sacrificed to invective or vision, and form can appear more a notation of performance than a stability of the printed page. Nevertheless, their speedy, inclusive fictions and figures constitute a memorably mistrustful, but still poignantly hopeful register of potential in Irish life. In the inspired accidents and collisions of Durcan's poems nuns give birth to the babies of priests, the Archbishop of Kerry has an abortion, a convention of the Catholic hierarchy in Maynooth bans colour photography, the Archbishop of Dublin films *Romeo and Juliet* in such a way as to ensure that the lovers never appear in the same shot together. The cussed, awkward, and politically subversive way in which Durcan's surrealism is in fact transparent to the actual realities of Irish social life has been made all the more manifest by the virtually un-satirizable absurdities and horrors of revela-tions in the 1980s and 1990s about the conduct of some members of the Irish Catholic clergy.

This poetry plays out its narratives and meditations across

almost the whole island of Ireland, particularly the rural Mayo of Durcan's parental origins and the provincial, bourgeois Cork of his sometime residence; but the city of Dublin is its most persistent topography. If Durcan defines himself in 'The Dublin–Paris–Berlin–Moscow Line' in *A Snail in My Prime* (1993) as 'a Dubliner | For whom Ithaca | Is Dublin Bay at twilight', it is with the traveller's Ulyssean knowledge of what 'Going Home to Mayo, Winter, 1949' from the earlier *Sam's Cross* (1978) calls 'the daylight nightmare of Dublin city'. The capital's cafés, galleries, pubs, churches, flats, parks, and public transport are frequently the locations of Durcan's caprices of imaginative transformation. In Bewley's Oriental Café in Westmoreland Street a security guard strips naked at Durcan's invitation; on a June afternoon in Stephen's Green Durcan wishes he was a woman, watching one 'riding | The clear waters of her cotton dress'; and in 'Making Love outside Áras an Uachtaráin' in *Sam's Cross* the speaker remembers himself and a girl doing exactly that—making love, that is, outside the gates of the mansion of the President of the Irish Republic in the Phoenix Park. Since the president at the time of this transgression was de Valera himself, the poem's final stanza imagines an outraged head of state approaching the lovers with murderous intentions:

> I see him now in the heat-haze of the day
> Blindly stalking us down;
> And, levelling an ancient rifle, he says 'Stop
> Making love outside Áras an Uachtaráin.'

The image of the old president of the Irish state levelling his rifle—kept, no doubt, since the 1920s—at the blissful lovers with the command that they stop doing what comes naturally and what brings delight has an energetically vituperative emblematic force: Durcan's poetry everywhere opposes that bleakly destructive, joyless negativity with its own licences and permissions. These include, memorably, such scenes of gratification and generosity as that figured in 'Teresa's Bar' in the volume of that title published in 1976: 'Where the air is as annotated with the to-bacco smoke of inventiveness | As the mind of a Berkleyan

philosopher' and where 'Outside in the rain the powers-
that-be | Chemist, draper, garda, priest | Paced up and down in
unspeakable rage.'

Another such power is the judge; and in the sequence 'Daddy,
Daddy' in the volume of that title published in 1990, Durcan
offers a quite extraordinary portrayal—at once deeply tender
and judgmentally baffled or even harsh—of his relationship with
his father, the 'President of the Central Court of the Republic of
Ireland'. The poet's distressed emotions of fear and hopeless
love are figured in this sequence as a narrative of marriage to,
'secret divorce' from, and a second marriage before death to the
father. The relations between erotics and power, and the erotics
of power itself, are thereby scrutinized as closely in this male
Irish poet's work as they are in Eavan Boland's, making it
unsurprising that Durcan has written, in 'The Haulier's Wife
Meets Jesus on the Road Near Moone', what Patrick Crotty
describes, provocatively, as 'arguably the strongest feminist
poem yet written in Ireland'.[15] In 'Daddy, Daddy', as a result, we
are given access to the psychology of an Irish High Court judge
who sympathizes with the IRA, a Fine Gael appointee whose
sole holiday in twenty-eight years has been to visit the home of
Mussolini. Durcan's humour, both destructive and corrective, is
therefore predicated on and grounded in his own home ground,
where he learnt how to say what his poetry now says to his father
in some of its most knowingly scandalous lines:

> Look into your Irish heart, you will find a German U-boat,
> A periscope in the rain and a swastika in the sky.

3. *Children of Limbo*

In the generation of Dublin writers which grew up in the 1960s
and 1970s the city has been newly and sometimes shockingly
made over into writing, notably by that group of poets, novelists,
and playwrights associated with the Raven Arts Press whose
founder, Dermot Bolger, himself one of the most significant of
these writers, edited a collection of essays by many of them,
entitled *The New Dubliners*, in 1990. The novelist Ferdia

MacAnna has acted as a kind of unofficial spokesperson for this generation in an essay in which he defines the bringing to light in this work of a hitherto hidden Dublin: that of the violent, drugs-infested, working-class estates of the northside.[16] The essay is sometimes hyperbolic in its propagandizing on behalf of these writers and also condescendingly, preeningly anti-academic; but it has great verve and is a useful place to begin an account of them.

Those named by MacAnna prominently include the poets Michael O'Loughlin and Paula Meehan, the novelists and play-wrights Bolger and Roddy Doyle, and also such figures as Sebastian Barry, Trudy Hayes, Anne Enright, Joseph O'Connor, and Aidan Carl Mathews. In their attempt to locate this 'new Dublin' in writing, MacAnna says, James Joyce is a figure of both fear and resentment: *Ulysses*, he says, is 'the nightmare from which Dublin is trying to awake'.[17] He claims—surely disingenuously—that many contemporary writers choose not to read it, and cites the case of Neil Jordan, who turned from writing to film-making in the attempt to cast off the long shadow of Joyce. Their models are likely to be instead, MacAnna insists, those of international writing and rock music, notably the late Phil Lynott of the Dublin band Thin Lizzy; and this new writing is read as 'Dublin's answer to American dirty realism—a kind of "Dirty Dublin Poetic realism"'.[18]

In MacAnna's own first novel, *The Last of the High Kings* (1991), Phil Lynott supplies the epigraph, and the style of its presumably semi-autobiographical comedy of adolescence derives not from Joyce's *Portrait of the Artist* but from J. D. Salinger's *The Catcher in the Rye*. Nevertheless, for all the postmodernist pluralism of MacAnna's essay, his own novel is actually about the confrontation between two Irelands: that of its hero Frankie in the mid-1970s—all punk rock and (paradoxically) fascination with things Californian—and that of his fiercely and opportunistically Republican 'Ma'. Frankie, her first-born, is, in her view, indeed 'descended from the High Kings of Tara' and, as such, destined to a future as, first, a Professor of History and, subsequently, President of the

Republic; whereas Frankie's ambition is actually to 'write a book, make a film or become a famous rock singer'. That MacAnna's own sympathies may be less clear-cut than his jauntily assured essay proposes is suggested by the novel's ending, in which Frankie's potential rebellion is in fact deflected by his unexpectedly passing his school-leaving certificate in English, Irish, and History—so that a Professorship of History may not be too unlikely a career outcome after all (even though it may, of course, be one whose brief includes the history of Phil Lynott). When Ferdia MacAnna himself toured Ireland with a rock band, his stage name was 'Rocky de Valera'. In satirical deviation there is inevitably an element of recognition or even of deference too. The real cultural break—the kind MacAnna advertises in his essay—would be simply no longer to care.

The Last of the High Kings is set in the well-off suburb of Howth, north of Dublin, and its family is a middle-class one. In Bolger and Doyle the locations are very different. Bolger is immensely prolific as poet, playwright, and novelist. His work is sometimes internally self-referential: moments, images, and situations are shared between the play *The Lament for Arthur Cleary* (1989) and the novel *The Journey Home* (1990), for instance. This makes for an imaginative intensity, even a claustrophobia, which is entirely consonant with his material, the reduced, trapped, and broken lives of the Dublin estate-dwelling working (or usually non-working) classes in their poverty, unemployment, drug-dependency, intermittent emigration, and homelessness. The word 'home' itself reverberates in Bolger, and his enquiry into what possible meaning it might have in these contexts supplies much of the energizing force of his writing. It also provides a grim perspective on an Irish present which, while it has grown away from all fruitful contact with its past, is nevertheless still shadowed by it in some of its deepest allegiances and instincts.

In *The Lament for Arthur Cleary* the eponymous hero is a returnee to his native Dublin who has spent fifteen years in Europe as a migrant labourer. On his return he discovers that the city of his upbringing has been almost entirely erased, morally as well as architecturally. Cleary is also, however, in the play's expressionist structure, a 'posthumous man', murdered because of his failure to understand how vicious the criminality of the city he has returned to actually is. Dead from the start of the play, then (like the characters of Brian Friel's *The Freedom of the City*), Cleary is predetermined in a way paradigmatic of his place and class. In *The Journey Home* the present narrative of the journey from Dublin to the West of Ireland of the young lovers Hano and Cait, fleeing the police who are seeking Hano for murder, is intercut with Hano's own story of how they have come to this point. A story of both his and Cait's fascination with the young Shay, who is also a migrant worker returned from Europe and eventually a murder victim, it has its melodramatic elements; but these pale in comparison with what it manages in the way of analysis and suggestiveness. In its opposition of the homo-erotically inflected, tender relationship between Hano and Shay to the depraved sexuality of two brothers of the Dublin political family the Plunketts (ironically named after one of the martyrs of 1916), it castigatingly explores some of the ways in which contemporary Irish politics is intermeshed with police corruption, black marketeering, and the illegal drugs industry. *The Journey Home* is itself a narrative in which this nexus of corruption destroys the lives of the young. To the venally opportunistic politicians they are Ireland's most valuable exportable commodity, its 'champagne'; but they appear to themselves to be the 'children of limbo' and 'internal exiles'. The latter is, damningly, the phrase used to describe those removed from their own home places—that is, the politically deracinated, exiled and probably about-to-be-killed—in Stalinist Russia.

The problematical nature of 'home' for all Bolger's characters is suggested first by their physical locations. Cleary's afterlife in *The Lament for Arthur Cleary* has him waiting at a railway station on a European border—in transit, nowhere—until he clears himself for departure by agreeing no longer to inhabit the dreams of the woman he has loved on earth. This ultimate act of selflessness—congruent, posthumously, with the life we have seen him living in the Dublin to which he returned—is also his

own ultimate self-destruction; and the play's metaphysical location overlaps very movingly with Cleary's actual, physical emigration and return, with the economic necessity which makes
him an exploited, rootless migrant. In *The Journey Home* the
lovers' flight from the police is just the final stage of an already
fugitive existence in which the transitoriness of dole queue,
emigration, and the flitting through the cheapest of northside
Dublin accommodations constitutes a perpetual urban restless-
ness and a perennially disadvantaged social mobility.

The concept of home in Dermot Bolger has, however, a more
extended application: it relates also to the search for an
Irish home, or nation, that might answer to the needs of a
deracinated, migrant generation still haunted by the assumptions and values of its rural and Catholic parentage and by its
Gaelic origins. This is sometimes figured intertextually, as when
The Lament for Arthur Cleary takes its title from, and alludes
several times to the great Irish eighteenth-century poem by
Eibhlin Dhubh Ní Chonaill, *The Lament for Art O'Leary*, in
which an Irish nobleman, husband of the poet, returns from
exile to an Ireland he can no longer understand, and is eventually killed as a result of his incomprehension (Bolger had made
his own contemporary version of the poem before writing the
play). It is also figured in the way an abandoned Catholicism
persists as a longing for the possibility of prayer and as an
explicitly theological language of sin and atonement. And it is
there too as a matter of defiantly locating contemporary experience in a historical continuum, as when Shay's battle-scars from
a fight on his Corporation estate in *The Journey Home* are
compared with those his grandfather got at the hands of the
Black and Tans. Bolger's point here, I take it, is not so much to
demythologize the past as to insist that the experiences of the
Shays of this world—reduced and deprived as they may appear—are as worthy of representation and record as those of the
soi-disant 'heroic' generations which preceded them, who may
well have behaved as they did in the expectation of producing an
Ireland very different from the one Shay must inhabit, but who
produced it none the less.

The desire for some concept of home which may measure up to present Irish reality finally founders at the close of the novel, however, in a parodistic revision of one of the central tropes of Irish nationalist mythology. The hero-narrator Hano has attempted, in his early youth, to discover in the West of Ireland 'some sort of identity or something', and he has met there an old woman who helps him generously in a quite unforeseeable way. At the end of the book, when his journey reaches conclusion and he is secure in the terrible knowledge that his arrest or death is imminent, he is again in this Sligo forest, being consoled by the old woman. She is clearly a terminal version of the Sean Van Vocht, the Poor Old Woman as a representative figure for Ireland; and this location of so much Irish mythologizing becomes for Hano a desolating, virtually apocalyptic image not of the Irish past but of its future as the servile playground of a new European financial élite, one from which the likes of Hano will be permanently excluded:

I used to think of here as the past, a fossilized rural world I had to fight to be rid of . . . But this crumbling house in the woods is the future, is our destination, is nowhere. I never understood it until now; soon it will be all that's left for the likes of you and I to belong to. City or country, it will make little difference, ruins, empty lots, wherever they cannot move us from.[19]

This is the projected terminal zero to which Irish history and tradition are brought in Bolger's impassioned and sometimes enraged prose; 'home' become a vacuum in which people in their 'own' places are only the expendable commodities of multinational capitalism. At the end of *The Journey Home* Hano 'knows' that he and Cait have just conceived a child. Knowing also that he will be absent from the child, given his own future-less future—which lies in death or imprisonment—he asks Cait to 'teach [the child] the first lesson early on: there is no home, nothing certain any more'.

In Roddy Doyle's work any sense of a specifically Irish history and identity is even further attenuated in its North Dublin Corporation housing-estate culture of rock music, drugs, alcohol,

Sky TV, football, and chips, and in its black-market economy
and permanent background of jobless, despairing vandalism. On
the estate of Barrytown the nationalist song 'A Nation Once
Again' is sung only during drunken celebrations of Ireland's
success in the World Cup, and with no more investment of
emotion than is placed in the other celebratory pop and football
songs also sung on the occasion. Similarly, where Bolger bestows
on his characters the dignity of a highly literary prose style,
Doyle reproduces orthographically the actual Dublin accents
and semi-literate stutterings of his, which include, again and
again, the use of four-letter expletives—in particular the
word 'fuck' and its cognates—but which are nevertheless vivid,
buoyant, and rich in inventive wit and humour. The novels are
almost as much novels of dialogue as the classic English upper-
middle-class novels of Henry Green and Ivy Compton-Burnett.
Doyle's triumph in his 'Barrytown trilogy'—*The Commitments*
(1987), *The Snapper* (1990), and *The Van* (1991)—is to reveal
this apparently debased culture and language as in fact the vehicle of great emotional range and depth, the powerful location—
even in its gaps, silences, and discontinuities—of tenderness,
affection, selflessness, and generosity. Without either condescension or sentimentality, he conveys the subtle inwardnesses
of lives in some ways inarticulately opaque to themselves—
although not so opaque in the case of one of them (in *The
Commitments*) that he cannot brilliantly define his kind as 'the
niggers o' Dublin', knowing that the Irish are anyway 'the
niggers of Europe'.

The family of the trilogy is called Rabbitte, which is a not
uncommon Irish name, but is also presumably a nod in the
direction of that superior middle-class condescension to, or fear-
ful hatred of the working classes which thinks of them as 'breeding like rabbits'. The plots of the three novels offer, as it were,
little isolated, temporary pastorals in the harshness of their characters' existences: the short-lived eponymous rock band, performing 'Dublin soul' (and modifying famous Black American
lyrics to give the songs a Dublin inflection) in *The Commitments*;
the daughter Sharon's pregnancy in *The Snapper*, which turns

her father, Jimmy Sr, into a 'new man' who frets more about the pregnancy than Sharon, and starts reading *Everywoman*; and the doomed business—a chip van—formed by the out-of-work Jimmy Sr and his friend Bimbo in *The Van*, where the termination of the business is also the termination of the friendship, to Jimmy Sr's intense distress. Doyle's main focus in these dialogue-novels is on the norms of Irish masculinity: in all three the plots reach a point where Irish men cry in public, and that ultimate breaching of taboo is at the core of Doyle's sympathetically but sceptically analytical fictions.

In his depiction of the overt *bonhomie* and toughness, the covert envy and tender-heartedness of Irish men, Doyle finely suggests the reservoirs of feeling within an apparent near-inarticulacy. In *The Van*, for instance, while both are watching soccer on television, his son Jimmy Jr tells Jimmy Sr that he intends to get married, and also that he is letting his father know before his mother. Jimmy Sr says only 'that's grand', but our awareness of his happiness for his son, his love of him, and his sense of the honour done to him by being the first to be told are all understatedly conveyed by the information that, when Liverpool gets a goal in the match which he is nominally watching, Jimmy Sr is not paying attention and has no idea who has scored. When, later in the novel, Ireland's World Cup success is the occasion of euphoric drunkenness in both Rabbittes, a moment of uniquely articulate intimacy occurs as they urinate together:

—I love yeh, son, said Jimmy Sr when they were letting go.
—He could say it and no one could hear him, except young Jimmy, because of the singing and roaring and breaking glasses.
—I think you're fuckin' great, said Jimmy Sr.
—Ah fuck off, will yeh, said Jimmy Jr—Packie saved the fuckin' penalty, not me.
—But he liked what he'd heard, Jimmy Sr could tell that. He gave Jimmy Sr a dig in the stomach.
—You're not a bad oul' cunt yourself, he said.[20]

This finely judged, perfectly pitched encounter reveals a tenderness of intimacy whose very inarticulacy is feelingfully articulate; and the unique moment of articulation is enabled by the euphoria of the culture of football—football, it might be said, as the poetry of the inarticulate. Or rather, in revealing inarticulacy as sometimes such a gentle and graceful thing, Doyle is offering the sense of delicate, complex, and subtle emotion under constraint; and the novels do have their (perhaps slightly hortatory) vision of an alternative: Rabbitte Sr's wife, Veronica, attends self-improving night classes, and their son Darren earns himself a place to read English at Trinity College Dublin. If Darren's education will eventually bring him to the point of literate articulacy which Roddy Doyle himself evinces in these novels, it must nevertheless remain an open question whether the selflessness of his finest feeling will ever equal his father's, 'uneducated' as that may be.

5

Ulsters of the Mind: The Writing of Northern Ireland

> Each person in Ulster lives first in the Ulster of the actual present, and then in one or other Ulster of the mind.
>
> (Seamus Heaney, 'Place and Displacement: Reflections on Some Recent Poetry from Northern Ireland')

1. Three Precursors

Introducing Sam Thompson's Belfast play *Over the Bridge* (1960) for an edition published in 1970, Stewart Parker said that 'if making "works of fiction" is not treated as an honest day's work in western society at large, in Northern Ireland it's scarcely countenanced as a furtive hobby'.[1] This is consonant with Derek Mahon's satirical evocation, in 1972, of 'that once birdless, if still benighted province'.[2] Nevertheless, since the late 1960s writing from the North of Ireland has come to be widely regarded as among the most significant contemporary work in the English language. Critics have ascribed this burgeoning to several factors: the unique spur to creativity given by a moment of extreme political tension and civil unrest; the rising into articulation, after the 1947 Education Act, of social classes which would previously have been tongue-tied by the lack of educational opportunity; the fortuitous coming together in the Belfast of the mid-1960s of a group of extremely talented individuals and the fostering of their work by a number of critics, literary editors, and publishers.

In fact, Parker's emphasis on the furtiveness of the act of writing in Northern Ireland prior to the later 1960s, while it undoubtedly reflects a socio-cultural reality for his generation, exaggerates the extent to which literature was not a significant

feature of the province's cultural life prior to that. To a certain
extent, it has taken the younger generation to put some of its
precursors more securely on the map of modern writing; and one
signature of contemporary Northern Irish writing is undoubtedly its generosity to an earlier generation: Seamus Heaney's to
John Hewitt (and to Patrick Kavanagh who, coming from Co.
Monaghan, belongs to the historical geopolitical province of
Ulster, if not to the post-Treaty configuration of Northern Ireland); Michael Longley's to Louis MacNeice and W. R. Rodgers;
Stewart Parker's own to Sam Thompson; and the frequent ad-
duction of the novelist Brian Moore, notably in Derek Mahon
and in Heaney's poem 'Remembering Malibu' in *Station Island*
(1984) which, dedicated to Moore, develops a contrast between
his present Pacific location—he lives in California—and the Atlantic Irish origin he shares with Heaney.

MacNeice's reputation has been decisively wrested by contemporary Northern Irish poets and critics from its relegation in
some English literary criticism, where it has waned in the
shadow of W. H. Auden's. In Paul Muldoon's long poem '7,
Middagh Street', in *Meeting the British* (1987), MacNeice actually figures as a character who, in a series of monologues, triumphs over Auden—also a character in the poem—in his view
of the relationship between art and politics, poetry and the
public life. Elsewhere too, MacNeice is admired for his evocations and analyses of the Belfast he came from, 'devout and
profane and hard'; for other treatments of the Northern Irish
landscape and cityscape (although it is undoubtedly western
rather than northern landscapes that predominate in his work);
and for his many vignettes of the inhabitants of the North, such
as 'The Gardener' whose soul when he dies goes off 'To find the
Walls of Derry | Or the land of the Ever Young'. A number of
younger writers, however, also read MacNeice, with a strong
element of self-identification, for his exile's love–hate relationship with the Ireland he left but constantly returned to, taking
stimulus from the sometimes irritated, sometimes affectionate
ambivalence of his attitude to his place, which, in 'Carrick Revis-
ited', he describes as one of 'our bridgeheads into reality | But

also its concealment'. As an Oxford-educated Ulsterman and Anglo-Irishman who spent most of his working life in London, MacNeice wrote into his work the crossed strains of his origins and career, offering hints, suggestions, and analogous cases, if not exactly models or templates, for a later generation also writing out of similarly crossed or stressed positions. Younger poets equally take lessons from MacNeice's tempered, unenthusiastic political scepticism which, resulting from his inwardness with Irish political complexities, prevented his ever making the overt alignments entered into by other—English—poets in the 1930s. MacNeice has become the name for desirable kinds of hybridity and plurality in a culture of positions often fixed into calcification.

Beyond this, there is the recognition among lyric poets who feel, in some sense, responsible to a world of ferocious political events, of MacNeice's ability to carry great 'freight' in the lyric, as one of his editors, Michael Longley, puts it;[3] although in this respect Yeats, and particularly the Yeats of the poems of the Irish Civil War in the 1920s, such as 'Meditations in Time of Civil War', has also, of course, been richly influential. MacNeice's 'Autumn Journal', however, written in London in the period leading up to the declaration of the Second World War, has, in this significant perspective, been a central poem. In its sixteenth section MacNeice voices an envenomed and un-illusioned account of his homeland which nevertheless registers in its detailed scrutiny the fascination of attraction as well as the repulsion of disgust. After a celebration of 'The linen mills, the long wet grass, the ragged hawthorn', the poem immediately turns to invective against the features of sectarianism:

> The land of scholars and saints:
>   Scholars and saints my eye, the land of ambush,
> Purblind manifestoes, never-ending complaints,
>   The born martyr and the gallant ninny;
> The grocer drunk with the drum,
>   The land owner shot in his bed, the angry voices
> Piercing the broken fanlight in the slum,
>   The shawled woman weeping at the garish altar.

John Hewitt's poetry has similarly been a resource for later writers. His career, extending from 1929 until 1986, covers a huge period in the modern history of Northern Ireland. Unlike MacNeice's work, therefore—he died in 1963—Hewitt's offers the spectacle of a poet actually attempting to cope with the increasing depredations of the province after 1968. His earlier work took its place as part of his public career as a socialist, meliorist, regionalist art gallery director, Protestant but usually—if always to some extent suspiciously—well-intended towards Catholicism.[4] Some of the most notable of his earlier poems, such as 'The Green Shoot', evoke a sectarian childhood only to pit its diminishments against a longing for release and alternative: 'I am the green shoot asking for the flower, | Soft as the feathers of the snow's cold swans.' In others, however, the insistence on rights to the land is phrased with a defensiveness which shades off into an insistence almost threatening, as at the end of one of his finest poems, 'The Colony'. Here, in something of the manner of Edwin Muir's historical monologue poems, a Roman colonist defines his user's entitlement to the land he has appropriated:

> for we have rights drawn from the soil and sky;
> the use, the pace, the patient years of labour,
> the rain against the lips, the changing light,
> the heavy clay-sucked stride, have altered us;
> we would be strangers in the Capitol;
> this is our country also, nowhere else;
> and we shall not be outcast on the world.

The fiction of the monologue, which manifestly allegorizes the Protestant planter's rights to the planted land in the North, may well have acted as inspiration for those numerous more-recent poems by younger writers in which geographical and historical analogies are found for the North. When Hewitt himself began to address the new Troubles, however, the scruple of his honesty and clear-sightedness compelled him to criticize exactly such allegorizing in his earlier work. In poems such as 'Parallels Never Meet' in *An Ulster Reckoning* (1971) he emphasizes the discontinuities and disproportions between past and present, metaphor and actuality: the figures of ancient Rome now 'trip and flounder in their togas' while

> the heartbreak remains,
> the malice and the hate are palpable,
> the flames authentic,
> the wounds weep real blood
> and the future is not to be foretold.

This self-revising self-chastisement is also a model for later Northern poets, in whom a questioning of responsibilities and obligations, and a suspicion of the ways in which suffering may be merely appropriated in poems, becomes itself the frequent focus of poetic attention.

Brian Moore is an immensely prolific writer whose career has extended from 1955, when he published his first novel, *The Lonely Passion of Judith Hearne*. Set in a run-down boarding-house in a once-prosperous but now increasingly seedy area of Belfast, and dealing with the emotional life of its eponymous heroine, whose circumstances are lower-middle-class shabby-genteel, the book presents a memorable picture of its time and place. A compelling study of urban, cultural, emotional, and sexual dereliction, it rewrites Joyce's *Dubliners* as an account of a paralysis of will maintaining its torpid entropy and stasis in 1950s Belfast. Moore finely evokes the city's defiantly myopic insularity and its deeply inscribed patterns of casual, almost unremarked sectarianism. In a Joycean way too, the novel offers a critique of the influence of the Catholic Church on the lives it scrutinizes: both Judith Hearne's sexless passivity, which veils strong sado-masochistic impulses, and which finds its outlet only in alcoholism, and the sexual desperation and thwartedness of the novel's returned American exile, James Madden, which culminates in rape, are ascribed at least in part to the Church's perverse attitudes to sexuality. As in *Dubliners*, the patient scrutiny cohabits with a scornfully satirical impulse. This book and some of its successors—*The Feast of Lupercal* (1957), set in a Catholic school in the 1940s, *The Emperor of Ice-Cream* (1965), set in wartime Belfast, *The Temptation of Eileen Hughes* (1981),

The Doctor's Wife (1988), and *Lies of Silence* (1990)—all dramatize in striking ways aspects of a Northern inheritance, although only *Lies of Silence* deals directly with the Troubles themselves.

In both *The Temptation of Eileen Hughes* and *The Doctor's Wife* Moore presents, in contradistinction to Judith Hearne, female characters triumphantly overcoming the submissiveness which has made them victims of male aggression, domination, or assumption. The 'temptation' to passivity is read as very deeply written into Northern Catholicism. Eileen Hughes is the victim of the thwarted and ultimately suicidal obsession of a failed priest; the 'wife' of *The Doctor's Wife*, Sheila Redden, is subdued by the Catholic bourgeois pieties and probities of her selfishly myopic husband. The novel includes, indeed, a hideous scene in which Sheila is raped by this enraged but apparently until then entirely decent husband, suddenly possessed by 'the unpredictable person inside of him'. The scene, in its horror but also in its presentation of a masculinity opaque to itself, crystallizes terribly the patterns of male self-pity, manipulation, and brutality which Sheila abandons in favour of a radically unpredictable life, leaving both husband and lover for an isolated singularity. The concept of the 'other life', whether that of sexual fantasy, adultery, or political or theological alternative, is a pervasive one in Moore; and it may be read as the expression of the desire contained by, but always threatening to disrupt the orthodoxies and narrowed certainties of a Northern Irish religious background.

The inexplicit but pervasive feminism of *Eileen Hughes* and *The Doctor's Wife* is accompanied by a delicate evocation of the ways in which the lives of both women have also been constrained by the Troubles: Sheila Redden, for instance, is alarmingly prey, even when in the arms of her lover, to memories and nightmares of a catastrophic Belfast bombing. These brief, restrained moments are actually more assured and telling versions of social disruption and psychological distress than *Lies of Silence*, a thriller set in 1980s Belfast and dealing with a kidnapping and car-bombing incident, which attempts a more comprehensive overview. The IRA gang is a clichéd one, the political motivation of terrorism is occluded in favour of a familiar and reductive psychopathological reading, and the feminist issue— elsewhere in Moore handled so delicately—is carried in an overtly, and consequently vulnerably moralistic or even didactic way. The novel's themes of betrayal, both sexual and political, are, as a result, uncomplicated by any real subtlety either of emotional or political feeling, and the book has, for all its suspense, a certain inertia and flaccidity. None the less, embittered exhaustion is itself worth expressing, and when the novel's hero Dillon, victim of a kidnapping, sees his Protestant neighbour leaving home, exhaustion rises to a coolly condemnatory and ramifying political rage, a potentially constructive anger which appropriates a Yeatsian lexicon ('mired'):

And now, watching him go off for his morning walk with his dog, Dillon felt anger rise within him, anger at the lies which had made this, his and Mr Harbinson's birthplace, sick with a terminal illness of bigotry and injustice, lies told over the years to poor Protestant working people about the Catholics, lies told to poor Catholic working people about the Protestants, lies from parliaments and pulpits, lies at rallies and funeral orations, and, above all, the lies of silence from those in Westminster who did not want to face the injustice of Ulster's status quo. Angry, he stared across the room at the most dangerous victims of these lies, his youthful, ignorant, murderous captors. What are they planning to do today, what new atrocity will they work at to keep us mired in hate?[5]

These novels of the place of Moore's origin, Northern Ireland, are accompanied in his *œuvre* by others—notably *Fergus* (1971), *Catholics* (1972), and *The Mangan Inheritance* (1979)—in which Irish exile is given one of its most mature and peculiar contemporary realizations, and in a way inflected by the specific stresses of Northern Catholicism, the religion which this novelist now decisively rejects. Moore—a Canadian, and then an American exile for most of his writing life—becomes the most striking modern Irish novelist of the trajectories of exile itself and of the pull both towards and away from the forms of Irish Catholicism among those born into it. In *Fergus* and *The Mangan Inheritance* Moore creates bizarre fictional structures—combinations of realism, fantasy, and allegory—in which the exile's dream persists disintegratively, or becomes a nightmare, even in those who make good, or a sort of good, and even into succeeding generations.

In *Fergus* the hero, a novelist trying to break into the lucrative but venal Hollywood market, is haunted by apparitions from his family and upbringing on the shores of Belfast Lough, including those of his father, mother, and own earlier self. The apparitions are a reminder of some of the tensions, envies, and humiliations of that earlier life, but they are also a setting of the compromises and collusions of Fergus's current existence against the moral absolutes of the Catholicism of his childhood. It gradually becomes clear to the reader that these are the hallucinations of extremity. Fergus is the victim of a heart attack and is presumably dying or dead during the course of the novel; Moore's style of lucid hallucinatory calm leaves it unclear what exactly is Fergus's state, but Terence Brown puts it well when he refers to Fergus's 'literally broken heart'.[6] In *The Mangan Inheritance* the failed American poet James Mangan goes to Ireland to search for his origins and to attempt to discover whether he is a descendant of the nineteenth-century Irish *poète maudit* much admired by Joyce, James Clarence Mangan. What he learns is a story of failure, brutality, and incest, of corruption extending through succeeding generations; and the novel offers a protracted deconstruction of many of the consolatory tropes of exile and myths of origin and return, in which the vacuous but persistent pieties and sentimentalities of Irish-American nostalgia are ferociously undermined. These books deal with ultimate crises of identity and self-knowledge, their central characters discovering who or what they might become, or who or what they have been trapped into being.

In both books too, the protagonist is prominently a writer and, on one of their several levels, the novels are allegories of the writing life. The Mangan 'inheritance' is both genetic and literary: the family curse ensures sexual as well as literary failure, and also that final requisite of the *maudit*, that he 'come to a bad end'. In *Fergus* the hero's hallucinations allegorize the way a writer is always elsewhere, in at least two places at the same time—the place of living and the place of writing—and the cost this exacts on those closest to him: 'Until now, he had thought that, like everyone else, he exorcised his past by living it. But he was not like everyone else. His past had risen up this morning, vivid, uncontrollable, shouldering into his present. How can I live a life with Dani, he wondered, if my mother keeps coming into the room?' Further, Fergus's hallucinatory father points out that the strength of the writer's desire for posthumous fame is, in Fergus himself, a substitute for the eternal life promised by Catholicism; and the novel leaves it open whether the hallucinations we witness are actually the only 'other life' Fergus is going to be given.

These strange combinations of realistic and non-realistic narrative in his mature fiction are an indication of one of the ways in which Moore's own texts often have 'other lives' too: they are intertextual with well-known pre-existent writing. Joyce is behind much of his work—the 'Circe' episode of *Ulysses* is an influence on Fergus's hallucinations, for instance; William Golding's *Pincher Martin* is probably a precursor of *Fergus*; the *doppelgänger* of Gothic fiction is manifestly an influence on *The Mangan Inheritance*, as are Grimm's fairy-tales and the Grail legend; and a version of *amour courtois* gone rancid operates as the central plot motif of *Eileen Hughes*. At the formal and structural level too, then, Brian Moore's books enact or even parade their own intrication in previous texts. Their examinations of exile and return, of origin and departure, of innocence and experience, of actual life and 'the other life'—whether of sexual fantasy, religious promise, or writerly fame—are themselves anchored in a crediting of simultaneity, alternative, otherness. In this, it could be said, they prefigure and then parallel a major anxiety in much of the other contemporary writing of Northern Ireland which is characteristically double-focused, turned in a Janus-faced way towards both form and event, prominently intertextual but vulnerably anxious about responsibility and obligation. When Seamus Heaney dedicates his poem to Moore, it suggestively crosses Ireland with America, the Pacific with the Atlantic, the actual with the imagined, the knowledge of what is 'welted solid to my instep' with the desire 'to rear and kick and cast that shoe'.

2. *Emblems of Adversity: Poetry after 1969*

There are some poems about Northern Ireland since 1969 which approach the 'situation' and its circumstances with an unapologetic decidedness and immediacy: probably the best-known of these is Thomas Kinsella's controversial *Butcher's Dozen*, an impassioned piece of polemic and invective published in the wake of the Widgery Report in 1972 which exonerated the British Army of guilt in the killing of thirteen Catholics in Derry city on 'Bloody Sunday', 30 January 1972. The poem's angry octosyllabics raise sarcasm to a higher literary power, as the dead victims of the soldiers' bullets speak, in a kind of parody of the Irish *aisling* or vision poem:

> Does it need recourse to law
> To tell ten thousand what they saw?

It is notable, however, that Kinsella is responding here as a writer from the Republic, and within an Irish nationalist tradition. His public rhetoric of outrage and indignation is a kind notably and, it may seem in some ways remarkably, eschewed by most of the poets of the North, in whom abrasiveness and outrage are often turned into something more complexly self-involving, if no less pained and dejected. Seamus Heaney, for instance, in one of his finest poems, 'Casualty', published in *Field Work* (1979), also runs his own response to Bloody Sunday and its aftermath through an imaginary conversation with the dead, but in a way which implies a self-doubting questioning of the whole concept of the poet's solidarity with a community: the poem is prominently preoccupied with the place of poetry itself as well as with the actuality of response to an appalling event. It is characteristic of some of the best poetry written out of the situation of the North that it proceeds with great tentativeness and hesitation before the implacable and intractable violence of its material; and when the poets comment on their work, it is often to assert the necessarily distinct realms inhabited by the poetic and the political, and to insist on the primacy of the imaginative act in the creation of the poem, however compelling the claims of 'responsibility' remain.

In the introductory essay to his second collection of prose, *The Government of the Tongue* (1988), Seamus Heaney maintains that in the early 1970s 'the poets did not feel the need to address themselves to the specifics of politics because they assumed that the tolerances and subtleties of their art were precisely what they had to set against the repetitive intolerance of public life'.[7] In fact, Derek Mahon, in an article written at the time, insisted that the real 'war' in Northern Ireland was between 'the fluidity of a possible life (poetry is a great lubricant) and the *rigor mortis* of archaic postures'. A good poem, he observed, in what has since become a much-cited remark, 'is a paradigm of good politics—of people talking to each other, with honest subtlety, at a profound level'.[8] A number of poems from Northern Ireland since 1969, notably Paul Muldoon's 'Lunch with Pancho Villa' in *Mules* (1977) and Tom Paulin's 'The Other Voice' in *The Strange Museum* (1980), themselves debate such matters, enquiring into the place of the poem in a fraught political context. The difficulty of reconciling the claims of poetry and responsibility is figured memorably in Heaney's 'Exposure' in *North* (1975), whose title puns on several senses of the word, one of which is the media 'exposure' given to the poet by those expecting that he will have something to 'say' about the Troubles. The end of the poem finds Heaney in entirely characteristic mood, 'weighing and weighing | my responsible *tristia*', where the Latin word aligns his predicament, ironically to some degree, with that of other poets called to public accountability: the Latin poet Ovid, who wrote a volume in exile entitled *Tristia*, and the Russian poet Osip Mandelstam, who became an internal exile under Stalin and took over Ovid's title for a volume of his own. The state of impasse to which these issues might lead is provocatively figured in two poems from different phases of Heaney's career, 'Viking Dublin' in *North* and 'Sandstone Keepsake' in

Station Island (1984), where he self-castigatingly ironizes himself as a kind of Hamlet incapable of decision or action, 'dithering, blathering', and 'not about to set times wrong or right'.

The problem for the poet in a time of great social and political upheaval is therefore not merely one of engagement with material: it is also, inevitably, a matter of form. John Montague's *The Rough Field* (1972) is explicit on the issue. This developing sequence about his own cultural and psychological background in Garvaghey, Co. Tyrone, written between 1961 and 1971, takes the stress of increasing political distress into its own compositional processes, noting 'The emerging order | of the poem invaded | by cries, protestations, | a people's pain'. One of the most focused statements of the issues, however, is Heaney's celebrated essay 'Feeling into Words', collected in his first volume of prose, *Preoccupations* (1980). After 1969, he writes there, defining his own gradual divorce from the assumptions of the 'New Criticism' in which he had been educated, 'the problems of poetry moved from being simply a matter of achieving the satisfactory verbal icon to being a search for images and symbols adequate to our predicament'.[9] The poet's aim, Heaney thinks, should be to discover what Yeats, in one of his poems responding to the other Irish 'Troubles' of the 1920s, called 'befitting emblems of adversity'. These would be, presumably, poetic figures and forms which might express feeling about 'the situation' with Mahon's 'honest subtlety', but which would also remain true to the compunctions, energies, and stresses of the poetic act itself.

What this frequently amounts to in practice is that the situation of the North since 1969 is located, in poems, in contexts of metaphor, figure, analogy, and allegory which provide the opportunity for the register of powerful, if sometimes unspecific feeling and for an attempt—oblique, unpresumptuous, and sometimes reticently unforthcoming—at understanding. The need to put the situation into perspectives of various kinds—to situate *it*, in fact—in ways that might allow honest, intelligent, and subtle but still feelingful response, is partly the reason that some individual volumes from the North in this period aim for a more inclusive and coherent structure than is attempted in the usual collection of separate poems. Montague's *The Rough Field* was an early and influential volume of this kind. An attempt to explore an inheritance, the sequence places images and narratives of Montague's childhood and youth in Garvaghey (the Irish *garbh fhaice*, translated as 'the rough field' of the poem's title) against evocations of the increasingly violent present, and sets the whole in a frame of marginal glosses from Irish historical and journalistic documents and reproductions of the woodcuts from John Derricke's *The Image of Irelande with a Discovery of Woodkarne* (1581), which present images of atrocity and military engagagement from sixteenth-century Ireland.

Such other volumes as Heaney's *North*, Tom Paulin's *Liberty Tree* (1983), Paul Muldoon's *Meeting the British* (1987), and Ciaran Carson's *Belfast Confetti* (1989) also propose themselves as coherent wholes, in which individual poems are complementary and interrelated. All seem to imply the impossibility, and undesirability, of single or certain response: they offer, rather, larger situatings, enquiries into symptoms and origins, trajectories of malaise. A similar impulse lies behind some of the many poetic translations of the period. In Paulin's *Seize the Fire* (1990), a version of Aeschylus' *Prometheus Bound*, for instance, and in Heaney's *The Cure at Troy* (1990), a version of Sophocles' *Philoctetes*, the ancient Greek narratives are made manifestly continuous or congruent with views of the contemporary fate of Northern Ireland. Michael Longley also frequently collapses the classical into the contemporary. 'The Butchers' in *Gorse Fires* (1991) offers a terrifying version of the conclusion of the *Odyssey*, when Odysseus murders Penelope's suitors and, in what seems a scandalously gratuitous act of revenge, hangs her maids. At the other extreme, his version of a poem by Tibullus called 'Peace' concludes in a dreamlike and erotic image of entranced desire, figuring the longed-for condition of peace as a sensuous woman who lets 'apples | Overflow between her breasts', where the manifestation of burgeoning natural process acts as a healing corrective to the poem's 'arms deals', 'war cries', 'skirmishes', and 'guerrilla tactics'. In Ciaran Carson's

First Language (1993) he translates episodes of Ovid's *Metamor-phoses* in a way that makes the violence of the original narratives metamorphose also into the situation of the North. The story of Persephone contains a 'hunger strike', and the story of Aurora and Memnon, which evokes the continuing embitterment of cultural memory (as in 'Remember 1690'), almost demands an Ulster accent:

> And every year from then to this, the Remember Memnon birds
>   come back to re-enact
> Their civil war. They revel in it, burning out each other.
>   And that's a fact.

These situating contexts and analogies are complemented in some of this poetry by others of more individual and pri-vate construction. A major element of Heaney's career is the discovery of various forms of 'emblematizing'. In what has been called the 'politicised linguistics' of *Wintering Out* (1973), for instance—a book deeply attuned to the meliorist Civil Rights moment of its composition—the English language as it is actually spoken in Northern Ireland is explored as the bearer of a long history of colonization, division, and tentative communication. In the elegiac pastoral modes of *Field Work* (1979), such as 'Casualty' and 'The Strand at Lough Beg', friends and relatives killed in the Troubles are movingly commemorated, even if the commemoration must cope with Heaney's wary uncertainty about the appropriateness of pastoral elegy to the material it handles here. In *Station Island* (1984) the poet self-punishingly imagines himself the auditor of the voices of the dead, which offer their own counsel on the relationships between art and atrocity, between the poem and the political moment; the returned ghosts include Colum MacCartney, the subject and victim of 'The Strand at Lough Beg', who now rebukes the poet for the 'saccharine' of the earlier elegy. This rebuke—which is, of course, a self-rebuke—is entirely typical of the self-doubt and self-revision of Heaney's poetry: the pressure to discover 'befitting emblems' is accompa-nied always by a besetting doubt about what, if anything, might ever 'fit' this occasion. Many of these anxieties are reflected, as we saw in Chapter 1, in Heaney's translation from the medieval Irish, *Sweeney Astray* (1983), and the accompanying 'Sweeney Redivivus' sequence of *Station Island*, in which his reinvention of himself as the poet-king Sweeney, who is transformed into an exiled and pursued bird, gives him images, emblems, and allegories of flight, chase, covert operation, and hunger which have clear congruences with the history of the nationalist community in the North, as well as with the plight of the poet himself, caught between mutually exclusive impulses and expectations.

Probably still his best-known set of emblems, however, is the one he discusses in 'Feeling into Words', his use of the photographs of Iron Age corpses preserved in the peat bogs of Jutland which he found in P. V. Glob's book *The Bog People* (1969). In a sequence of poems initiated by 'The Tollund Man' in *Wintering Out* and continued and brought to fulfilment in *North*, which have come to be known as Heaney's 'bog poems', he meditates on these sacrificial and ritual killings as analogues for various atavisms, including those of the Irish republican tradition. In the most powerful poems of the sequence, such as 'The Grauballe Man' and 'Punishment', Heaney disturbs very dark emotions within his own responses to these emblematic figures, enunciating what appears an almost 'tribal' set of loyalties, affinities, and complicities, and exposing exacerbated feelings which are physical, even sexual, as well as political. Although he has been criticized for some of the implied attitudes here, and for an apparently static and ritualized sense of historical process, there is no doubting the urgency, entrancement, and seriousness of address in this work. The conclusion of 'The Tollund Man' offers a chastened and deeply saddened self-image which may also stand as a paradigm of the way many contemporary poets of Northern Ireland attempt a crossing of strains, locations, cultures, and periods in the desire to discover memorable and permanent forms which maintain a proper probity—without sententiousness or hyperbole or self-advertisement—in relation to their dreadful material:

> Out there in Jutland
> in the old man-killing parishes
> I will feel lost,
> unhappy and at home.

That Heaney's sequence of 'bog poems' should have originated in his contemplation of photographs has its appropriateness, since after 1969 the people of Northern Ireland were
suddenly compelled constantly to contemplate journalistic and
televisual images of themselves and their places for the first
time: 'each vibrant scene | Translated to the drizzling screen', as
Derek Mahon puts it in 'Derry Morning'. Mahon's best known
poem, 'A Disused Shed in Co. Wexford', offers the surreal image of a 'flash-bulb firing-squad' of photographers disturbing a
cluster of mushrooms waiting in a dank shed in the Republic
'since civil war days'; the poem is dedicated to J. G. Farrell,
whose historical novel of the Irish 1920s, *Troubles* (which I
discuss in Chapter 2), may have been significant in its genesis.
Lifting their heads 'in gravity and good faith', the mushrooms
plead that the photographers might 'speak on their behalf'. This
compelling motif is not necessarily coextensive with the suffering brought by the 'situation' in the North: indeed, its potential
is to ramify in a great pathos of applications (the poem itself
refers to the 'lost people of Treblinka and Pompeii'). However,
the relationship it proposes between intrusive and potentially
appropriative or exploitative photographer and hidden, bur-
dened, and virtually inarticulate—or at least inaudible—subject
is manifestly congruent with that of poet and victim in the
Northern Irish context.

Mahon's work frequently itself figures the tiny area of compe-
tence which poetry may presume in relation to the sufferings of
a violent history. In 'Rage for Order' he transforms Wallace
Stevens's late-Romantic concept of the poet's 'blessed rage for
order' in his poem 'The Idea of Order at Key West' into something much more sceptically dejected and self-disgusted:

> Somewhere beyond the scorched gable end and the
>   burnt-out buses
> there is a poet indulging

his wretched rage for order—
or not as the case may be; for his
   is a dying art,
an eddy of semantic scruples
   in an unstructurable sea.

This ironizing of the potential scope of poetry is itself, however, also ironized at the end of the poem, where the speaker knows he will soon have need of the poet's 'desperate ironies'. It is at what might well seem this virtual vanishing-point of ironic contact between poetry and history that Mahon's own work proceeds: its distilled residue of emotion is permitted only by being veneered in self-mistrust. This sometimes takes the form of setting a violent history in large temporal or mythological perspectives, as in 'The Snow Party' in the volume of that title published in 1975, which imagines the piercingly pure civility of a ritualized Japanese social event brutally cut across by an 'elsewhere' in which 'they are burning | Witches and heretics | In the boiling squares', and in 'The Last of the Fire Kings', where a myth derived from J. G. Frazer's anthropology, in which tribal kings are ritually slaughtered by their successors, is reinvented so as to become the opportunity for an end to the killing rather than a perpetual recurrence of it.

Among the most compelling of Mahon's perspectives are those which set the Belfast of his childhood in a context of other more manifestly colonial situations—the seventeenth-century Holland of 'Courtyards in Delft', for instance, and the twentieth-century Algeria of 'Death and the Sun (Albert Camus, 1913–1960)'. In the former, Mahon dreams himself into a famous painting by Pieter de Hooch in an evocation of shared backgrounds of cultural and psychological repression awaiting their end. The Delft of the painting—bourgeois, Protestant, and swept clean—and the Belfast of his own childhood equally await the furious 'Maenads' of apocalypse. In 'Death and the Sun' Camus is commemorated as the focus of Mahon's adolescent intellectual passion; and, as such, he becomes also the focus of a meditation on a Belfast which 'never imagined the plague to come', as the inhabitants of the Oran of Camus's allegorical novel *La Peste* also fail to imagine the plague that descends on them. In both of these poems an ultimate self-referential irony operates, since great works of art are themselves read anew for what they might say of, or to, Mahon's own history and place. They are disintegrated and reconstituted as elements of Mahon's own wretched rage for order, which celebrates the way poems and paintings may become, in unpredictable ways, the vehicles of contemporary understanding. If the poet remains hopelessly 'beyond the scorched gable end and the burnt-out buses', he may nevertheless, from that position, read, and write, new, self-authenticating interpretations of political conflict.

The poem of a childhood in which sectarian division is apparent, but contained, features also in a number of other poets. Tom Paulin has several variations on the theme, including 'In the Lost Province' which wonders 'Who would dream of necessity, the angers | Of Leviathan, or the years of judgement?' His exploration of his Ulster Protestant heritage and identity attempts to account for these necessities and angers in various different forms as his career has developed, but frequently, as Bernard O'Donoghue has said, by 'making one historical event the matrix of another (like a medieval typologist)'.[10] This produces poems like 'Liberty Tree' in the volume of that title, in which Paulin's ideal of a civilized eighteenth-century republican politics, the 'dream | of that sweet, equal republic', which met its fate in the savagely repressed uprising of 1798, is celebrated as a valuable, if utopian, desire in present debased Irish political life. It also produces the dense layering of historical epoch upon epoch in the long poem 'The Caravans on Lüneberg Heath' in *Fivemiletown* (1987), which yokes together the Thirty Years War and the poet Simon Dach with the career of Martin Heidegger in Nazi Germany and, by implication, the long contemporary war in Northern Ireland. The poem constitutes an ambitious attempt to identify a particular Protestant European heritage in the contours of crucial moments of its intellectual, political, and aesthetic history.

The same volume also offers, in several poems, something quite exceptional in Northern poetry: the voicing, in a series of dejected, insecure, and subliminally violent monologues, of the contemporary loyalist mentality. In such poems as 'Mount Stewart' and 'Fivemiletown' the matrix for contemporary Northern history becomes not so much another historical event as a sexual event: the plight of lovers in scenes of sexual subjection and rejection acts as a coded, tacit, and taciturn allegory for a politics of desuetude and desolation and for the feeling of being entrapped or constantly under surveillance. These poems may be ghosted by Seamus Heaney's more straightforwardly allegorical 'Act of Union' and 'Ocean's Love to Ireland' in *North*, which read Ireland's relationship with England in sexual terms; but, if so, they take on an altogether individual quality of taut, edgy inwardness. Many of Paulin's poems also use meditations on architecture as the focus of a reading of Ireland's politicized landscape: an eighteenth-century mansion, Joyce's Martello Tower, a holiday cottage, and army surveillance towers are all scrutinized until they release intimations of the way history has scarred locality and human lives. In Paulin's adventurously experimental work a political intelligence is alive in a poetic way, buoyantly catching its inspiration among the flotsam and jetsam of the world, conveying the impression that virtually anything it fixes on may take its place in a kind of illuminatingly ragged patchwork.

In this, it has come to share something with the work of Paul Muldoon, the most apparently zestful of all contemporary Northern poets. From the precocious beginning of his career, with *New Weather* in 1973, he has steered clear of any of the obvious kinds of engagement with the North, in an *œuvre* provocatively full of vanishings, evaporations, mysterious disappearances, and metamorphoses. One of his poems describes a hare's 'singleminded swervings'; and it may well be thought that something of the kind is his own procedure too. Incapable of standing still, his poems flit nervously but directedly among preoccupations, categories, and modes, offering an idea and an ideal of the poem as the site of transformation and hybridity.

Muldoon rings many changes even in his shorter poems. In the constantly allusive and sophisticated 'Gathering Mushrooms' in

Quoof (1983), for instance, he weaves together memories of his father, the experience of hallucinogenic drugs, and—most strikingly, in the poem's conclusion—a response to the IRA hunger-strikes of 1981, in which ten internees in Long Kesh (The Maze) prison died. The effect, multiple and complex, is to enable a genuinely sympathetic reaction to the prisoners' suicidal decision without any sympathy for what Muldoon would almost certainly consider the atavistic and tendentious politics which provoked it. He also invents more capacious long forms for himself in such poems as 'Immram' in *Why Brownlee Left* (1980)—discussed in Chapter 1 above—'The More a Man Has the More a Man Wants' in *Quoof*, '7, Middagh Street' in *Meeting the British*, the title poem of *Madoc* (1990), and 'Yarrow' in *The Annals of Chile* (1994). In all of these, weird, fanciful, and apparently haphazard juxtapositions, collocations, and conjunctions become the principles of narrative form and also the principles of, as it were, the deconstruction of narrative form.

One of the most prominent of these conjunctions, since his first book, has been a crossing of Irish history and mythology with a well-informed knowledge of the history and mythology of Native Americans; and in 'The More a Man Has the More a Man Wants', the tale of Gallogly, a man on the run in Ireland, engaged in covert activity of some never-fully-specified kind, is crossed with the tale of an Apache or possibly an 'Oglala Sioux' Indian, and with a variety of other American material too. The whole is also interlarded with references to numerous further narratives of stealth, pursuit, and flight, promiscuously including the medieval poems *Gawain and the Green Knight* and *Buile Suibhne* (the poem Heaney translates as *Sweeney Astray*), Robert Louis Stevenson's *Kidnapped*, Lewis Carroll's *Alice in Wonderland*, the Trickster narratives of the Winnebago Indians, the cartoons of Yogi Bear, and Chuck Berry's song 'Johnny B. Goode'. It is virtually impossible to say exactly what all this nimble poetic footwork adds up to; but Muldoon has clearly been reckoning up some of the ways in which a poem might avoid the pitfalls of received opinion or conventional expectation. One thing the poem manifestly does add up to is a space in which the clichés of the reportage of violence can be undermined, as in this instance of what something fails to 'add up' to after an explosion:

> Once they collect his smithereens
> he doesn't quite add up.
> They're shy of a foot, and a calf
> which stems
> from his left shoe like a severely
> pruned-back shrub.

This refuses to flinch from the recognitions necessary to its object: the poet's gaze steadies itself by maintaining an almost cruelly unfeeling evocation of actuality. Yet—paradoxically, it may be—the horror of the thing is more unforgettably caught than in many more apparently feelingful responses. In the contexts of political and journalistic cliché about Northern Ireland, such a poem draws a moral strength from being one of the very few places where this kind of scrupulous and punctilious exactitude may be shaped. In 'The More a Man Has the More a Man Wants' a novel kind of poetic decorum unpresumingly discovers the blackly ironic gap between the actuality of physical violence and any linguistic representation of it.

Muldoon's coruscating intertextuality is complemented in contemporary Northern poetry by Ciaran Carson's textual variations on oral Irish cultural forms, notably the digressive story-telling or yarn-spinning of the *seanachie* tradition, in his three mature collections, *The Irish for No* (1987), *Belfast Confetti* (1989), and *First Language* (1993). His buoyantly or even boisterously long lines carry jokes, nostalgias, velleities, Proustian evocations of memories and sensations with a carefully manipulated impression of improvisatory panache; but they also sustain a grim poetry of terrorized urban abasement and disintegration. Their material is, prominently, bombings, shootings, knee-cappings, internment, enforced and voluntary emigration, insanity. By imitating Irish narrative voices, these poems manage to record even the darkest matter with a grimly or stoically black humour, and they always catch their material up into the speedy onward impulse of their narrative and dramatic logic and illogic. This makes them one of the most accurate poetic witnesses to the pressure and texture of Belfast street life as it has been lived, or endured, since 1969. They retrieve individual and communal histories from deeply meditated topographical, psychological, and cultural sources. The poems therefore manage the large aim of defining the contours of a social and psychic map of the city, in a way that suggests that Joyce's evocation of Dublin in *Ulysses* has acted as a rich source of possibility for Carson. In these narratives the poet becomes an obsessive cartographer and tally-keeper, the loving and despairing preserver, in writing, of what is always disappearing and metamorphosing in reality, as terrorist attacks and army architecture and surveillance keep the city in a constant state of erosion, disturbance, and 'renewal':

> And I am the avenging Archangel, stooping over mills and
>   factories and barracks.
> I will bury the dark city of Belfast forever under snow:
>   inches, feet, yards, chains, miles.

This forbidding image, in 'Slate Street School' from *The Irish for No*, of the poet as the exacter of vengeance on the city itself for exacting such savage acts of vengeance on its own opposed communities, is one disconsolate way a poetry might proceed in contemporary Northern Ireland. A virtually opposed image is offered in the work of Michael Longley, in which everything seems either to nerve itself to a fraught and agonized contemplation of violence, or, more frequently, to envisage some deeply desired, if only vaguely apprehended and figured alternative to it. The poems in which Longley most directly confronts the circumstances of atrocity are notable for the very odd, sometimes surreal angles and perspectives of their approach. In 'The Linen Workers', from *The Echo Gate* (1979), a particularly gross act of carnage, in which ten people were massacred, is memorialized in the same poetic act in which Longley elegizes his own father: the private grief, as it were, licenses and authenticates the public witness, so that the grief seems taken deeply into the poet in a way designed to avoid the possibility of the appropriative or exploitative. Both private and public feeling are themselves, however, set under the distancingly surreal perspective of the poem's opening line, 'Christ's teeth ascended with him into heaven'. That zany but minatory image is the means by which both father and linen-workers enter the poem: the father's teeth are remembered in their bedside glass, and a set of dentures falls to the ground after the massacre. The poem, as it were, permits itself the memorial and elegiac tone only by first setting the terms of its own extraordinary imaginative contract.

Frequently, however, Longley's poems figure any engagement with the situation more remotely, by what we might think of as another kind of 'translation', in which palliatives for distress and exacerbation are tentatively discovered in forms of vegetation. 'The Ice-Cream Man' from *Gorse Fires* offers, in response to news of yet another sectarian murder, simply a punctilious itemization of the vegetation seen on a trip through the Burren, the area of outstanding beauty and botanical interest in Co. Clare. The poem offers the beautiful listing of flowers as a substitute for the ice-cream man's now forever vanished list of flavours; and, in refusing to do or say anything more, in a way that is dignified as well as helpless, the poem plaits, almost literally, its memorial wreath. It is unsurprising, then, that in 'Finding a Remedy' in *The Echo Gate*, Longley defines his own pacific art as one devoted to 'bringing together verse | And herb, plant and prayer to stop the bleeding'. It is a moment in Longley which very tentatively and unpresumingly promotes the idea of poetry as the salve for psychic or social distress; and it chimes harmoniously with Seamus Heaney's impatient but convinced insistence in 'The Settle Bed' in *Seeing Things* (1991) that

> whatever is given

Can always be re-imagined, however four-square,
Plank-thick, hull-stupid and out of its time
It happens to be.

3. *Forms and Deformations: The Novel after 1969*

If the poetry of Northern Ireland since 1969 has been, in the main, a poetry of obliquity, the novel in the same period has been much more straightforwardly addressed to the situation itself and to the issues it raises. This is true despite the fact that the best novels of the Troubles are very varied in style and kind. They include the realism of Jennifer Johnston, Bernard MacLaverty, and Deirdre Madden; the postmodern inter-textuality of Benedict Kiely, Robert McLiam Wilson, and, to some extent, Glenn Patterson; and the commandeering of the genre fiction of the thriller in Brian Moore and Ronan Bennett. There is the strong sense in these novels that the subject of the North must be addressed in fiction, even if necessity and compunction are matched by an equally strong, and articulate, feeling of incapacity or hopelessness. It is also notable that, in what we might think of as the third generation of Northern writers, those born in the 1960s, the novel rather than the poem or the play appears to have become the most significant and energizing form.

Jennifer Johnston redeploys the modes of elegantly economic realism used in her 'Big House' novels in *Shadows on our Skin* (1977) and *The Railway Station Man* (1984) to produce books in some ways continuous with the effort and effect of those novels but also directly addressed to the quite different specificities of the violence in Derry city in the early 1970s and the machina-tions of the IRA in the early 1980s. The plots of both derive, as do those of her Big House fictions, from dangerously transgres-sive relationships. In *Shadows on our Skin* the Derry Catholic schoolboy Joe, who, like some of the heroines of her Big House books, is a putative poet, and whose brother Brendan is a mem-ber of the IRA, forms a relationship with his teacher Kathleen, who is engaged to a British soldier; and in *The Railway Station Man* Helen Cuffe, whose husband has been murdered in error by the IRA, forms relationships with the two men she meets when she moves to the West of Ireland, the war-wounded Englishman Roger Hawthorne, and the local Damian Sweeney, a messenger for the IRA. In both books the transgressions propose frail, transitory emblems of consolatory *rapprochement*, but they nevertheless culminate in the catastrophe of physical violence and murder. As in Johnston's Big House novels, the realms of the personal and the political are terminally collapsed into each other; and the terrorist event happens almost casually as a feature of the ebb and flow of family life, domestic circumstance, heredity, and heritage. *The Railway Station Man* makes one of its political points by aligning Roger Hawthorne's sense of 'the needless dead' of the Second World War—such as those killed in Dresden—with the dead of Northern Ireland. His insistence that the state has its terrorism too is part of Johnston's own insistence on the complications and confusions of motivation, desire, and involvement which should corrupt any stereotyped conception of 'terrorism'; and these novels draw their strength from Johnston's long engagement with transgression, *rapprochement*, and catastrophe in Irish history.

In the realistic modes of Bernard MacLaverty's novels too, which share a style of luminous but understated intensity with his short stories, the attractions and risks of transgression are the organizing principles of plot. In *Lamb* (1980), a novel obliquely related to the Troubles, the Catholic religious brother Michael Lamb kidnaps the epileptic Owen Kane, one of his charges in an Irish Borstal school, taking him to London as the only conceivable alternative to the life of casual brutality and repression he is forced to endure at home. The novel climaxes when, with nowhere left to turn, Michael takes Owen to the west of Ireland—frequently the scene in Irish writing of a desired alternative existence—and drowns him there. The culture which has produced this psychopathology is heavily implicated in the Troubles of the North, since the brother in charge of the Borstal, Benedict, is a Republican with strong links to the IRA.

The novel to a large degree occludes the sexual quality of Michael's interest in Owen. The mythical parallel it invokes, after Joyce, is that of Daedalus and Icarus, which reads Michael and Owen as father and son rather than master and ephebe. If this makes the ethical issues less problematic, the transgressive relationship itself has great pathos and force: Michael and Owen transgress, indeed, into a relationship which has strong overtones of the *doppelgänger*, since Michael's surname, 'Lamb', is, we are told, the translation of the Irish 'Owen'. In this sacrifice of the Lambs, therefore, we may read a realism aspiring to the level of the allegorical. The book's dark paradox crosses the private story with a national resonance, as Michael meditates on the hopelessly fated trajectory of his ideal: 'He had started with a pure loving simple ideal but it had gone foul on him, turned inevitably into something evil. It had been like this all his life, with the Brothers, with the very country he came from . . . The good that I do is the evil that results.'

In *Cal* (1983) a sexual liaison is given prominence as the element of transgression, since the young working-class Catholic of the title falls in love with the librarian Marcella, the Catholic wife of an RUC man whose murder he has been involved in. The story of their affair has an excellently realized quality of edgily tender *rapprochement*; but, in its ultimate transgression, it has its dark *doppelgänger* elements too, notably when the near-destitute Cal dresses in the clothes of the dead policeman. When he thinks of them as his 'hair shirt', in an allusion to the self-inflicted sufferings of the pious Dubliner Matt Talbot, and, further, when the novel includes a number of references to the appalling suffering depicted on the Grünewald *Crucifixion*, we realize that the theme of transgression has become, in this novel, the medium of a deeply Catholic study of guilt, expiation, and the desire for confession, forgiveness, and absolution. The actual vocabulary of Catholicism is invoked often, as when Cal fears that the closer he gets to Marcella the more likely he is to tell her the truth, 'to commune with her and be forgiven', where the verbs activate Catholic concepts of the sacraments of the eucharist and penance. The novel's power derives from its wavering perspectives: it is itself both implicated in, and judgmental about the sado-masochistic cultural forms it anatomizes and inhabits. Its final sentence brilliantly yokes the implication and the judgement together. When Cal is arrested, we are told, 'he stood in a dead man's Y-fronts listening to the charge, grateful that at last someone was going to beat him to within an inch of his life'.

It is unsurprising that the North should provide such opportunities for realistic fictions and that it should also supply the means of imaginative extension for some of these writers. The psychologies and narratives of transgression, victimization, and betrayal, and the plots of personal, familial, political, and religious entrapment with which they are taken up, are given a unique edge and focus by this material, but such things, of course, supply the plots of numerous other realistic fictions too. It may seem more surprising that the North has also produced, particularly in the 1980s and 1990s, a more experimental, or postmodern, kind of writing, in which the circumstances of the situation disturbingly persist, but now in alignment with dislocating literary structures and forms. These are 'dislocating' in some literal senses: the locations of the North are put into alienating perspectives by being viewed from other locations, and ways of writing about the North are sceptically scrutinized and weighed by being juxtaposed intertextually with other kinds of writing.

In Benedict Kiely's *Proxopera* (1977) and *Nothing Happens in Carmincross* (1984), situations of suspenseful terror are crossed with numerous references to Irish and popular song, mythological, legendary, and historical material, and other literature, to create a complex interweaving of material. The violence is therefore evoked in structures that attempt to command it in the discipline of form and order, but which nevertheless ironically register their own incapacity. The consciousnesses at the centre of both books—in *Proxopera* the old man Binchey forced to carry a terrorist bomb by proxy, in *Nothing Happens in Carmincross* the historian Mervyn Kavanagh, visiting Ireland from America for the wedding of his niece, whose murder forms the terrible climax—are both intensely literary and mnemonically associative. These very self-aware novels consequently take their shape from the debate articulated early in *Carmincross* between Kavanagh and his friend Burns about the nature of allusion and the structure of history:

From a mind mouldy with overmuch reading, he tells Mr Burns, every experience takes the form of a quotation. Mr Burns argues, though, that every experience is a quotation and that every quotation is a renewed experience, a light switched on again in a darkened room to reveal familiar objects. Mervyn recalls that Marx suggested that history repeats itself, the second time as farce. Marx was too kind. History is farce the first time. God only knows what it is, the next time round.[11]

Nothing Happens in Carmincross is itself a historical novel, published in 1984 but set in the North of the early 1970s, and permissively employing anachronism. The relationship posited between 'experience' and 'quotation' is therefore made all the more problematic. The already-writtenness of the place is unnerving, and the dangers of cliché, of the exploitation of material, of mere repetition, and of the sententious are so large that the writer who would do the situation justice must tread very warily indeed. Kiely's wariness in *Carmincross* places his hero, Kavanagh, in the position of dislocated exile: his return is to the scene of his childhood, but this is a scene placed in a new perspective for him by the years away. Both intimate with his place, and radically estranged from it, therefore, he situates it revealingly. The novel's plot takes the form of a postmodern picaresque, in which Kavanagh moves through adventures in Ireland on his drive to his home in the North, accompanied by a lover, Deborah (there are explicit references to the flight of the mythical Irish lovers Diarmid and Grainne). The lovers are pursued by Deborah's violent husband, and the violence of men towards women forms a constant accompaniment to the political violence. The narratives of homecoming, flight, and pursuit—all of them inextricably woven into past narratives—finally fracture hideously as the atrocities pile up towards the end of the book and the culminating explosion happens in Carmincross, Co. Armagh. Kavanagh's role as returnee assumes a tragic dimension when it is he who accidentally takes the warning call of the terrorists, too late to act on it. The returned exile is therefore plunged to the very heart of the vortex of the violence of his homeland; and the explosiveness of the end of the book, in which many others besides Kavanagh's niece die, is all the more overwhelming to the reader as a result of its delayed detonation. In *Nothing Happens in Carmincross*, as in Brian Moore's *The Mangan Inheritance*, the trope of the exile's return in Irish literature is itself turned inside out: the desired dreamland of original piety and affection has become a nightmare madhouse, just as what T. S. Eliot called the 'simultaneous order' of a literary tradition has become a confused, frenetic, and deconstructive riot of proliferating reference and allusion, finally coming to seem less a way of placing the present in perspective than a pathological gibbering to hide the reality of desolation.

In its intense allusiveness, *Nothing Happens in Carmincross* is matched by Robert McLiam Wilson's *Ripley Bogle* (1989). For most of its length the book takes the form of the subjective narrative of its destitute eponymous Belfast hero as he wanders the streets of London. Since, although destitute, he is also a brilliant Cambridge literary dropout, his narrative refers frequently to other literature, notably the work of Dickens and Orwell, but in fact stylistically it is an extraordinary amalgam of elements of Joyce, Beckett, and Nabokov. Ripley is like one of Beckett's intellectual tramps, but he speaks (despite his obscenity) more with the brio and swank of Nabokov's self-entranced monologists and, like some of them, he is a liar; and the book includes a pastiche of the 'Circe' episode of *Ulysses*. The story Ripley tells is as extraordinary as that of Beckett's Molloy or Nabokov's Humbert Humbert; and, as in *Molloy* and *Lolita*, what we gradually realize we are witnessing is the revelation of a pathology. Ripley has suffered the usual depredations of a Catholic, working-class, Falls Road childhood, and his story, told in flashbacks, is an excellent evocation of that world, as rich in topographical and atmospheric density as the poetry of Ciaran Carson. Even more than Mervyn Kavanagh's story, Ripley's slowly reveals his inability to escape his past. The pathology is one he is alert to when, as the child of Welsh and Irish parents, he names himself 'Ripley Irish British Bogle', and mocks the various categories of Irishness on which Catholic nationalism and Republicanism thrive.

If there is a culturally schizoid element in this self-definition, Ripley's own psychological near-schizophrenia mirrors it. The pain Ripley actually dwells on during the novel returns him again and again, in imagination, to a dreadful abortion scene which takes its place in an almost explicitly Catholic critique of what he calls 'the pornopulse of modernity'. However, it is only towards the very end of the book, when the novel's repressed narrative returns with a vengeance, that we discover the ultimate cause of his mental and physical disintegration. He has been forced to act as the decoy while an old schoolfriend is shot by the IRA, and he is subsequently stranded for hours on an unmoored boat while the friend dies a slow and ghastly death. Ripley's swaggering monologue therefore comes, in retrospect, to seem the braggadocio of a man whose style is evolved to protect himself from the despair of this knowledge. The postmodern poise and panache of the book shelve suddenly into a chasm of naked distress; Ripley's guilt shadowing permanently what he still wishes, self-deludingly, to regard, in the novel's final word, as his 'aplomb'. The point of his writerly autodeconstructions is that there is no fictional method equal to this story: its distress cannot be contained by form, just as he cannot himself be contained by the forms of civilization (Cambridge, most notably) which he tries on, or tries out. What the novel's own form appears to intend is that the social deformations of the Falls Road cannot be assuaged by any of the forms of English prose narrative.

In the work of Glenn Patterson the dislocations are, first of all, a matter of narrative perspective. In *Burning Your Own* (1988) which is, like *Nothing Happens in Carmincross*, a historical novel, the Belfast of the catastrophic summer of 1969 is viewed through the eyes of the 10-year-old Protestant child Mal who enters into a strange, compelled relationship with the outcast Catholic boy Francy Hagan. The disaster of the narrative, in which Francy is eventually burned to death when he petrolbombs his own shelter (giving the book's title the most hideous of its many ironic relevances to the story), makes the novel a sort of *Lord of the Flies* of Belfast which offers itself to symbolic or allegorical readings. The conflagration marks the initiatory moment of the larger conflagration of the North itself in that year: 'by that July in 1969 it seemed that just about everybody in Northern Ireland was going to be sorry.' *Fat Lad* (1992) presents, like Kiely's *Nothing Happens in Carmincross*, an exile's return. Drew Linden has left Belfast for an English university education; his return, as the assistant manager of a bookshop, is the prelude to the unfolding of a Protestant family history extending back beyond Partition. The novel is therefore a narrative of locations and dislocations. The network of entanglements, the complex of loyalties and betrayals, of affection and violence, in this family also acts as a metaphor for, or an analogue of the political violence of the province on Drew's return; and his own contact with the violence, through the murder of a friend and through his relationship with a woman whose boyfriend has been killed by an army Saracen tank, provide the book with crucial elements of its plot.

Patterson's dislocating perspectives are the origin in his work of a kind of limpidly hyper-realistic style, constantly moving into levels of historical density and into the figurative and symbolic. In *Burning Your Own* Francy is an entirely credible Belfast working-class reject, but he is also a quasi-mystical or shamanic figure, a dark *genius loci* deeply conversant with Belfast history, topography, and lore. The book is both a densely realized account, from a child's perspective, of some of the significant moments of 1969 and a more symbolic meditation on childhood, friendship, belonging and exclusion, tribal complicity, and individual conscience in a context of exponentially increasing violent sectarianism. Similarly, in *Fat Lad*, the fact that the novel is both personal and public story is signalled by its title, which is Drew's childhood mnemonic for the six counties of post-Partition Ulster; and the Linden family story becomes both a means of evoking definitive moments of Protestant working-class history and of giving expression to the usually occluded histories of women, who are seen as subversively undermining,

even while officially supportive of Protestant male prerogative.
These histories, largely of entrapment and repetition, are memorably emblematized by the grotesquely swollen family goldfish
which, even when released for exercise into the bath, still swims
only in circles. This emblematizing is accompanied by elements
occasionally more radically unexpected in their figurative implication, as when the unique act of love-making between Drew
and Kay, the Catholic woman who has obsessed him, becomes
lushly utopian, the crossing of many kinds of border. This is an
'act of union' too, which provocatively urges a politics from its
sexuality, even if it does so in a slightly hyperbolic manner:

What was involved was a supporting cast of family, lovers, friends
disposed collusively about this island and the next and the continent
beyond . . .

Vast movements of peoples were communicated in the silence of a
single kiss. Borders were crossed, identities blurred. Land masses rose
and fell with their bodies.

Not surprisingly, their lovemaking was long and intricate and when it
was over they felt the moment ebb away into the future.[12]

Towards the end of *Ripley Bogle*, when the plot in which he is
inextricably entrapped has come to seem to Ripley himself altogether too melodramatically already-written, he fears that his
story might have started to sound 'like the worst kind of thriller-
writer bullcrap'. Because the thriller, on television and in
movies, as well as in prose, has been one of the most prominent
modes of representing Northern Ireland since 1969 in popular
culture, it is unsurprising that novelists like McLiam Wilson
should feel shadowed by it. Ronan Bennett's *The Second Prison*
(1991), along with Brian Moore's *Lies of Silence*, actually engages it in an attempt to shock the popular genre into a newly
perturbing authenticity, both psychologized and politicized. In
the subjective narrative of the IRA cell leader Kane, told in
convincingly disturbing flashbacks from his English prison, the
novel offers a convincing psychology of terrorism, neither sympathetic nor hostile, but concerned to offer an account of its
cultural and political conditioning and dedicated to the disruption or deconstruction of stereotype. The episodic flashback

technique here, familiar enough in thriller form, seems deeply appropriate to the life it records, which is itself fragmented and dislocated as the result of frequent incarceration in a Northern Irish internment camp and in British prisons. Through some of the standard plot manœuvres of the thriller we are given a compelling sense of the terrifying erosion of familial and personal attachment in Kane's life, and of the oscillating claims of responsibility. As in several other novels of Northern Ireland, betrayal, both personal and political, becomes the crucial pivot of plot, and Kane's final opting to end the cycle of revenge-killing in which he is involved is accompanied by an equally difficult decision to leave the woman he loves to the man he has taken her from. Kane explicitly denies that he feels 'redemption' in this selflessness, but nevertheless, as in *Cal*, his use of the word means that the terms of Catholic theology are never far away from the psychological analysis.

The 'second prison' of the novel's title is the prison of the past in which its many characters are also immured. Kane eventually frees himself from this prison by the force of his own will and conscience, along with the moral prompting of the women he associates with: his barrister ex-girlfriend, his present barrister, Harriet Cockburn (probably modelled on Gareth Pierce, the defence counsel in the case of the Birmingham Six), and his lover Kate. One way in which this is a revisionist thriller is in its prominent preoccupation with gender: the implosively macho world of Kane's Belfast background is gradually extended by his alternative relationships with women. This is contrasted with the movement deeper and deeper into the second prison by Kane's opponent in the novel, the deranged, psychotic policeman Tempest. Wounded in Belfast, he dedicates the rest of his life to ensuring the deaths of all of those in Kane's IRA cell apart from Kane himself, who nevertheless witnesses the spectacle of Tempest's final murders and suicide. The novel's interrogation scenes between Kane and Tempest pit high intellect against high intellect, and in the shared intimacies of their self-knowledge and of their knowledge of each other the book proposes a dark kinship between terrorist and policeman, between the state's dominance through violence and the terrorist's knowledge of the structures of power. The sense of near-*doppelgänger* intimacy is cemented when Kane (and we as readers) eventually learn that Kate is in fact Tempest's estranged wife. The novel extends its generic structures until they memorably accommodate a subtle study of the border territories between freedom and manipulation, love and loss, loyalty and betrayal.

4. *Give Me Your Answer Do: Theatre after 1969*

For all its variety, then, the novel of Northern Ireland returns almost obsessively to a number of themes and tropes: the often stressful or violent configurations of family life; the conflicting tugs of loyalty and betrayal, of solidarity and individual conscience; exile and return, location and dislocation; relationships in various senses transgressive; images of entrapment and isolation; the psychology of victimization; the tendency to make use of the terms of Catholic theology as a means of defining patterns of psychology, motivation, and behaviour. It is the exceptional combination of this intensity of preoccupation with an adventurous variety of means that gives the novel of Northern Ireland a large part of its claim on our attention. There is a willingness to push form to newly perturbed accommodations with the exceptionality of this material; and in the best of the drama of the North the same holds true. The Northern Irish theatre in this period extends from the realism of the work of Graham Reid, most notably the *Billy* plays of the early 1980s, a television sequence which explores the patterns of domestic and political violence in a Belfast Protestant family with a sensitively tender insider intimacy, to the intense expressionist stylization of Frank McGuinness's *Observe the Sons of Ulster Marching Towards the Somme* (1986) and *Carthaginians* (1988) and Anne Devlin's *After Easter* (1994), which finds in the quasi-religious visions of its lapsed-Catholic central character Greta a compellingly pitiful figure for contemporary Irish suffering. The Troubles have featured both directly and obliquely in the theatre of Northern Ireland; some plays, such as Devlin's earlier *Ourselves*

Alone (1985), engaging in an almost agitprop way with the realities of social and political life; others, such as the work of McGuinness, Brian Friel's *The Freedom of the City* (1974) and *Volunteers* (1979), and Stewart Parker's *Spokesong* (1975) and *Catchpenny Twist* (1977), searching for metaphors, suggestive analogies, allegorical resonances, and significant emblems.

Some of the difficulties of realism as well as some of its strengths are apparent in Reid's *Billy* sequence. For all the scrupulous honesty and humour with which it portrays its thwarted family lives, its figuring of an alternative is managed only in the very terms it elsewhere criticizes as part of the problem. Father and son, who have been deeply hostile to each other throughout, come to a tentative *rapprochement* at the end of the sequence only by joining together in an act of physical violence against others. It appears here that Reid is himself locked into the violent macho tropes of which he offers a critique elsewhere in the sequence. Devlin's *Ourselves Alone* explores the possibilities of a feminizing of the Sinn Fein motto which supplies its title, and paints a credible portrait of lives which have undergone politicization even in their smallest and most intimate details—'the only loyalties you are allowed are ideological', says Josie, the pregnant daughter of the play's violent patriarch, Malachy; but, like the *Billy* plays, it too fails to escape a certain sentimentalizing of family relationship. At its close Malachy agrees to protect Josie, in a way hopelessly inconsistent with the characterization we have been offered up to that point. Both plays indicate something of the struggle realistic theatre has in Northern Ireland when it attempts to articulate alternatives rather than to portray pattern and stasis. It is, nevertheless, instructive that plots should turn so persistently on generational conflict and the slender possibility of its resolution.

Stewart Parker's *Spokesong* and *Catchpenny Twist* are bravely experimental and wonderfully eloquent plays. They take some of the mechanisms of the revue—music, song, dance, stand-up comedy, quick-change artistry, trick cyclists, vocal

trios, and four-piece bands—and turn them towards an articulation of Northern Irish history, bigotry, terrorism, and violence in
quite unpredictable and deeply ironic forms. The ex-school-
teachers of *Catchpenny Twist*, who become a song-writing team,
gradually learn that in contemporary Northern Ireland everything, even their own acknowledged 'catchpenny idiocies' (torch
songs for female vocalists along with cynically Republican
broadsheet ballads), may become sucked into the vortex of
vaguely paranoid terrorist fantasy: the song-writers end up as
the blood-bespattered victims of a parcel bomb, having been
mistakenly thought collusive with the British Army intelligence
network. The effect is of a musical revue gone berserk, taking on
far more than it was ever intended to bear as it spine-chillingly
mixes its media, turning comic routine into terror, joining together in the same postal delivery an invitation to a European
song contest and the live bullets of a terrorist murder threat,
sliding the lyrics of pop song—'there's somebody out there'—
into the statement of panic.

In the remarkable conceit of *Spokesong* the history of the
bicycle in Belfast is crossed with a reading of the situation in the
early 1970s, in a way that is no doubt knowingly referential to
the well-known bicycles in the work of Samuel Beckett and
Flann O'Brien, but that lends them an entirely new implication.
The play begins and ends with the singing of the Edwardian
popular song 'Daisy, Daisy, give me your answer do' ('You'd
look sweet | Upon the seat | Of a bicycle made for two') and
brilliantly releases its complex themes of history, family,
generational conflict, and religious identity from a reading of the
song's tale of love and bicycles. The different histories of the
bicycle in *Spokesong*—those of pre-combustive locomotion, of
childhood competitiveness, and of adolescent sexuality—are
figured as an alternative to the public history of the First World
War and the current war in the North. To Frank, bicycle-shop
man and hero of the play, public history is only 'depraved folklore', whereas real history is 'all the things that ordinary people
do with their time': 'A bicycle hides nothing and threatens noth-

ing. It is what it does, its form is its function. An automobile is a weapon of war.'

However, as in *Catchpenny Twist*, this internal history is both collusive with, and victim of an external or public history: in this play too there is a literal explosion, and there is also the figurative explosion in which Frank is forced to overcome a sentimental attitude to the past. His bicycle shop is taken over by the schoolteacher Daisy, daughter of a Republican but mistress of her own destiny. Accepting Frank's offer of a tandem, she is orienting herself and this bicycle shop of Ireland towards an alternative future predicated neither on Frank's nationalist sentimentality nor on his adoptive brother Julian's outsider cynicism, but on her own bravely single-minded political and sexual revisionism: Daisy's 'answer', indeed.

In Seamus Deane's view, the trajectory of Brian Friel's whole career is formed by his responses to the North: *Translations* (1981), in particular, is read as 'a parable of events in the present day'.[13] *The Freedom of the City* and *Volunteers*, however—both plays of the early 1970s—are the only works of his which directly take the Troubles as their material. In the former, three civil-rights marchers in Derry city find themselves accidentally immured inside the mayor's parlour in the Guildhall after a so-called riot has been dispersed by the RUC. In fact harmless and unarmed, they are nevertheless shot by the Army when they emerge. The play's movement towards this climax is framed by their own posthumous speeches, the reactions of others—an Army brigadier, a journalist, a sociologist—and the speeches of the English judge who eventually sits on the tribunal held to inquire into the circumstances of the killing which exonerates the Army. The play has its manifest connections with the killing of thirteen civilians by the Army on Bloody Sunday in Derry in 1972 and with the subsequent report of the Widgery Tribunal— the incidents commented on by Kinsella in *Butcher's Dozen*, as we have seen. In *Volunteers* a group of IRA internees is on daily release from prison to take part, voluntarily, in an archaeological dig in a city site, of which this is the last day (the city is unnamed, but controversial digs were taking place in Dublin's Wood Quay area in the early 1970s). They are despised by their fellow internees for agreeing to work and, as the play develops, it becomes clear that they will be savagely punished—probably killed—on their return to prison. The play centres not only on the relationships between the men and those they work with, but also on the symbolic associations that accrue to the recovered skeleton of a Viking, christened 'Leif'. *Volunteers* is dedicated to Seamus Heaney, and there appears to be some crossing between its archaeological interests and emblems and Heaney's own in *North.*

In both plays Friel's experimental structures act as powerful theatrical metaphors in which political feeling is rendered emotionally concrete rather than emotively propagandist, although the plays undoubtedly carry a strong propagandist charge too. In *The Freedom of the City* the circumstances of life in Derry city for the deprived Catholic population, and their powerlessness before the forces of state control, are perfectly figured by the theatrical coup in which they are dead on stage as the curtain rises and the story of their reaching this catastrophe is acted out retrospectively. Friel's ear for the actualities of Irish vernacular speech has never been better than it is in this play; and the impotence of the characters is finely figured by the way their rich Derry speech is gradually erased by the official discourses—military, forensic, academic, journalistic, republican-balladic, ecclesiastical—into which it is then translated. The play presents us with the sad reduction that is their afterlife, when they are dragged down into the tawdry interpretations and ideological falsehoods of others. *The Freedom of the City* thereby devastatingly ironizes the sense of promise and reward normally carried by the phrase that forms its title.

In *Volunteers* the play's title, which suggests both the willing nature of the work the prisoners are undertaking and, of course, their status as republican soldiers, is similarly undercut by the revelation of the largely involuntary way they have been brought to this point. Friel's central metaphor, that of the murdered Viking who can be interpreted as anything an individual character wishes to make of him, is a very resonant one, joining together the actuality of violent death and the processes of cultural retrieval and transformation in a way that brings the play's themes into harmony with much of the rest of Friel's work, and that also possibly implies some reservation about the potentially dangerous acts of interpretation being made by this very play itself.

Both plays contain a similar character: Skinner in *The Freedom of the City* and Keeney in *Volunteers* are malcontents, wits, lively analytic intelligences, mockers, and, in Keeney's case, explicitly a Hamlet-like adopter of an 'antic disposition'. Both see the reality of their respective situations in ways hidden from the other, less intelligent or more well-meaning or deluded characters: Skinner knows that the occupants of the Guildhall will be punished for their acts of 'presumption' and 'sacrilege'; Keeney is the one who tells the others about the prisoners' kangaroo court which has sentenced them all, and he is also the one who compels them to realize the 'imbecility' of refusing to recognize themselves as victims. Much of the moral and political authority of the plays is therefore invested in these characters; and the controversial reception of the plays tends to focus on critical responses to them. Skinner dies regretting his characteristic 'defensive flippancy', and in the knowledge that 'to match their seriousness [that of the British state] would demand a total dedication, a solemnity as formal as theirs'. *The Freedom of the City* ends with the burst of automatic fire which kills all the characters—but they remain standing, in a concluding tableau.

If this ending represents something very close to an endorsement by Friel himself of the necessity for a violence to match the violence the characters are victims of, the force of Keeney's characterization in *Volunteers* pulls in the opposite direction. Skinner becomes, as it were, a member of the IRA in the moment of his death, whereas Keeney all but renounces his past commitment as he approaches what will probably be his. The story he invents about Leif is the story of a 'subversive' committed to a cause for all the wrong reasons; and, while Keeney admires the 'consistent passion fuelled by a confident intellect' of another internee, he recognizes in himself 'the inability to sustain a passion, even a frivolous passion'. His outburst about the others' reverence for the figure of the victim poses the play's central political issue at its most acute: Keeney's indecisive frivolity is the result of his knowledge of how close 'volunteer' might be to 'victim', of how the attachment to a cause may disguise the impulse to sacrificial martyrdom. In presenting both positions with the clarity of adequate context, Friel is uncondescendingly non-judgmental, and these plays are, as a result, very powerful political theatre.

That Frank McGuinness is sceptical about such political theatre may be inferred from the fact that, when a play-within-a-play figures in *Carthaginians*, it is clearly a parody of exactly such Irish theatre, from O'Casey to Friel (the characters, for instance, are all called Doherty, like Lily in *The Freedom of the City*). *Observe the Sons of Ulster Marching Towards The Somme* also includes a play-within-a-play; and the prominence of theatrical self-referentiality of this kind in McGuinness is one index of the system of historical and literary intertextuality that informs his work more generally. In *Observe the Sons of Ulster* he takes— boldly and riskily, for a Catholic and native of the Republic— one of the crucial moments of modern Northern Irish Protestant history: the devastation of the 36th (Ulster) Division on the Somme during the First World War when 6,000 men were killed. The eight characters take part in the battle of 1 July 1916, the anniversary of the Battle of the Boyne in 1690; and the commemorated Protestant victory is crossed over, in the memory of the survivor, Kenneth Pyper, with his memories of the Somme battle itself, which becomes for him a fight for 'freedom of faith'. He is aided in this process of historical parallel by the fact that several of the men, who come from various Ulster counties and have representative Ulster trades (blacksmith, weaver, miller, shipyard worker, preacher), have also been part of 'Carson's Army' (the Ulster Volunteer Force), the paramilitary unit formed to oppose Home Rule in 1913. The deaths on the Somme, consequently, which are already much rewritten and mythologized, become in *Observe the Sons of Ulster* the vehicle for an engagement with some of the ways in which Northern Protestant or loyalist history acts as a radically conditioning force on contemporary politics; and the play engages with this at the visceral level at which it actually operates, rather than at the level of analytic abstraction at which it tends to persist in other types of interpretative discourse.

The linkage between the experience of the Ulster Division and contemporary Ulster loyalism acts as the impetus to a study of the psychopathology of embattlement, entrapment, and the struggle with, or the subjection to ancestor-worship. The play is also much preocupied with ideas of cause, covenant, and confraternity; and, in relation to the latter, it has a prominently homo-erotic element. In fact, *Observe the Sons of Ulster* transforms the homo-eroticism endemic to the literature of the First World War into something intricately both testing and consolatory, an aspect of the patterns of sectarianism apparent in the soldiers' behaviour, but also partly modifying, or even destructive of them. In the homo-erotic relationship between Pyper and David Craig, McGuinness has found an emblem that joins extreme cultural embitterment to the possibility of an alternative personal tenderness and hope. Although the relationship itself does not survive the apocalypse of the Somme, its unsentimental utopianianism holds the possibility of converting the violent red hand of Ulster into the red self-inflicted wound on Pyper's hand which Craig bandages in one of the play's most vivid moments. A play about the struggle with 'ancestry' of various kinds, *Observe the Sons of Ulster* offers the tentative hope that, at least in an alternative form of male sexuality, where self-sacrifice might coexist not with military, nationalistic, or sectarian ideology, but with affectionate eroticism and sympathy, the darkest of the old gods might die. A very great deal lies behind the simplicity of Pyper's words to Craig as he goes out to die: 'I've learned to want you.' Which is why, I assume, the play concludes by turning a battle-cry into a dance.

In *Carthaginians* the destitution of the characters who inhabit a graveyard in Derry city—which for all of them is a consequence of the Troubles and particularly of the deaths of Bloody Sunday—is crossed with a structure of classical reference which acts neither heroically nor mock-heroically in any of the usual ways, but rather as a system of mobile paralleling and undermining of the kind that also forms the historical parallel in *Observe the Sons of Ulster*. Virgil's *Aeneid* (and the music of Purcell's *Dido and Aeneas*) are dramatic intertexts in the play, which contains a Dido who is a 'queen' in the homosexual rather than the regal sense. The intertexts make it plain that this burial ground in Derry, with its Beckettian rising pyramid of 'disposed objects', is an underworld not altogether unlike Virgil's in Book VI of the *Aeneid*. It is the site, in particular, of a number of hesitant tendernesses between the despised, the outcast, the rejected, and the mad. Presenting itself fairly clearly as a Catholic play to complement the Protestant *Observe the Sons of Ulster*, *Carthaginians* also offers an inside-out version of the Virgilian imperial theme. The character Paul who builds the pyramid of rubbish speaks of the 'foreignness' of Derry, although he was born there, describing it as part of the Roman empire: 'I live in Carthage among the Carthaginians, saying Carthage must be destroyed, or else—or else— . . . I will be destroyed.' As part of the surreal quiz show he conducts from time to time during the course of the play, he then asks 'Who wrote *The Aeneid*?' and answers his own question: 'An Irishman wrote it.'

This is as oblique a phrasing of nationalist resentment against British imperialism as the writing of Northern Ireland offers, and it must contend with the question another character, Hark, asks Dido: 'Is the united Ireland between your legs? The united Ireland's your disease.' Nevertheless, the play's system of disrupted allusiveness finds a compelling metaphor for the desire that some genuine alternative might come into being when it manifests a Virgilian hope that the dead might rise. The characters are waiting in the graveyard for the return of ghosts, with the knowledge that, as one of them puts it, 'we must tell each other the truth. For us all to rise again.' That 'rising' may be sexual as well as political and eschatological, since the play's play-within-a-play features not only cross-dressing but cross-connecting too: it is about the 'mixed marriage' of Catholic and Protestant. *Carthaginians* implies that this sort of rising, in which the 'united Ireland' may well actually lie between people's legs, might provide Derry with the opportunity to become a 'new city', which is said, in the play, to be the definition of the word 'Carthage'. If this is one of the meanings waiting to be read out of the suggestive representations of *Carthaginians*, its conclusion certainly raises the dead of Derry in the most literal sense, when the characters recite the names of the thirteen dead of Bloody Sunday. In a moment of quite unsentimental pathos, they accompany their recitation with Walter de la Mare's poem 'The Travellers', which makes reference to a 'host of phantom listeners', and they conclude with a prayer for forgiveness, with its instruction to 'bury the dead . . . raise the dying . . . wash the living'. The following, final stage direction is, in effect, a short prose poem:

Light begins to break through the graveyard's standing stones. At first its beam is narrow, golden and strange, like a meeting of the sun and moon. Birdsong begins. The light increases in power, illuminating them all. The birdsong builds to a crescendo. Looking at each other, they listen, in their light.[14]

5. An Afterwards?

An IRA ceasefire—fragile, unstable, and since rescinded, as I write in April 1997—was declared in September 1994. If the poets were slow to respond to the war, they were quick to respond to the possibility of peace. Michael Longley, in 'Ceasefire' in *The Ghost Orchid* (1995), returns to the Homer he had translated in 'The Butchers': not now to the *Odyssey*, however, but to the ending of the *Iliad*, the moment when the old king Priam weeps with the younger Achilles who has killed his son, Hector. This 'ceasefire' concludes with Priam's speech of forgiveness:

> 'I get down on my knees and do what must be done
> And kiss Achilles' hand, the killer of my son.'

In 'Tollund' in *The Spirit Level* (1996), which he dates 'September 1994', Seamus Heaney returns to Jutland and the place again seems reverberant with the associations of home. Registering both familiarity and strangeness, as his 'bog poems' in *Wintering Out* and *North* had done in the early 1970s, this new poem figures not the stasis and repetition of the earlier sequence but the possibility of change and renewal, imagining Heaney and his companion as

> ghosts who'd walked abroad
> Unfazed by light, to make a new beginning
> And make a go of it, alive and sinning,
> Ourselves again, free-willed again, not bad.

Just over two years later it is to be hoped, against hope, that this time the poets have not spoken too soon.

Notes

Preface

1. See Seamus Deane, *A Short History of Irish Literature* (London: Hutchinson, 1986) and Bruce Stewart, '"Anglo-Irish Literature", *moryah*', *The Irish Review*, 14 (Summer 1993), 88–93, 93.

2. Stewart, ibid. 89.

3. Thomas Kinsella, *The Dual Tradition: An Essay on Poetry and Politics in Ireland* (Manchester: Carcanet, 1995), 111.

4. This is the term usually used of the guerilla warfare which led to the end of British rule in (part of) Ireland, although in the revisionist history of recent times it has sometimes been seen as a patriotic, nationalist term which glamorizes and heroizes at the expense of historical actuality. In such history the term is therefore sometimes demoted to lower case—the 'war of independence'.

5. See Dillon Johnston, *Irish Poetry after Joyce* (Notre Dame: University of Notre Dame Press, 1985).

6. See Terence Brown, 'Yeats, Joyce and the Irish Critical Debate', in *Ireland's Literature: Selected Essays* (Mullingar: The Lilliput Press, 1988), 77–90. The theatrical and critical activities of Field Day are described and analysed in Marilynn J. Richtarik, *Acting Between the Lines: The Field Day Theatre Company and Irish Cultural Politics 1980–1984* (Oxford: Clarendon Press, 1994).

7. Seamus Heaney, 'Introduction' to the William Butler Yeats section of Seamus Deane (ed.), *The Field Day Anthology of Irish Writing*, ii. 783–90.

8. W. J. McCormack, *Ascendancy and Tradition in Anglo-Irish Literary History from 1789 to 1939* (Oxford: Clarendon Press, 1985), 241.

9. See David Lloyd, *Anomalous States: Irish Writing and the Post-Colonial Moment* (Dublin: The Lilliput Press, 1993). In opposition to that, I am thinking particularly of Edna Longley's work. See especially her 'Introduction: Revising Irish Literature', in *The Living Stream: Literature and Revisionism in Ireland* (Newcastle upon Tyne: Bloodaxe Books, 1994), 9–68.

10. David Perkins, 'Literary Histories and the Themes of Literature', in Werner Sollors (ed.), *The Return of Thematic Criticism* (Cambridge, Mass.: Harvard University Press, 1993), 109–20, 113.

Chapter 1

1. James Joyce, *A Portrait of the Artist as a Young Man* (Harmondsworth: Penguin, 1992; first published 1916), 204, 205, 274.

2. See his introduction to *Finnegans Wake* (Harmondsworth: Penguin, 1992).

3. See, for instance, Robert Welch in his introduction to W. B. Yeats, *Writings on Irish Folklore, Legend and Myth* (Harmondsworth: Penguin, 1993). It is nevertheless the case that Yeats's famous essay 'The Celtic Element in Literature' is deeply indebted to Arnold.

4. Cited in J. C. Beckett, *The Anglo-Irish Tradition* (London: Faber and Faber, 1976), 131.

5. W. B. Yeats, 'A General Introduction for My Work', *Essays and Introductions* (London: Macmillan, 1961), 520.

6. Brian Friel, *Translations* (London: Faber and Faber, 1981), 43.

7. See Sean Connolly, 'Translating History: Brian Friel and the Irish Past', in Alan Peacock (ed.), *The Achievement of Brian Friel* (Gerrard's Cross: Colin Smythe, 1993), 149–63.

8. A translation by Joan Trodden was published in 1984.

9. In the original Irish the poem's title translates as 'The Language Question'. The pun on 'issue' is therefore all Muldoon's. I am grateful to Patrick Crotty for this point.

10. Seamus Heaney, *Preoccupations: Selected Prose 1968–1978* (London: Faber and Faber, 1980), 138.

11. Although Heaney's indecision about this kind of usage in his own work—a peculiar indecision, in my view—is signalled by the way he revises this line in his *New Selected Poems 1966–1987* (London: Faber and Faber, 1990) into 'There you once heard guns . . .'

12. Edna Longley, *Poetry in the Wars* (Newcastle upon Tyne: Bloodaxe Books, 1986), 222.

13. I say 'particularly since the Revival' because scholars are increasingly paying attention to earlier efforts at translation by Samuel Ferguson, for instance, whom Yeats had studied, by James

Clarence Mangan (1803–49), and by more obscure figures such as Charlotte Brooke (?1740–93) and James Hardiman (1782–1855).

14. 'The Divided Mind' is reprinted in Mark Storey (ed.), *Poetry and Ireland Since 1800: A Source Book* (London: Routledge, 1988), 207–16.

15. Thomas Kinsella (ed.), *The New Oxford Book of Irish Verse* (Oxford: Oxford University Press, 1986), p. xxvii. Kinsella presents his views at greater length in *The Dual Tradition: An Essay on Poetry and Politics in Ireland* (Manchester: Carcanet, 1995).

16. See Clarke's note in his *Collected Poems* (Dublin: The Dolmen Press in association with Oxford University Press, 1974), 547.

17. John Montague, *The Figure in the Cave and Other Essays* (Dublin: The Lilliput Press, 1989), 52.

18. Cited in *The Poems of Tennyson*, ed. Christopher Ricks (London: Longmans, Green and Co., 1969), 1280, n. 105.

19. *The Figure in the Cave*, 52.

20. Robert Graves, *The White Goddess* (London: Faber and Faber, 1961), 455.

21. See Anthony Cronin, *No Laughing Matter: The Life and Times of Flann O'Brien* (London: Grafton, 1989).

22. Samuel Beckett, *First Love* (London: Calder and Boyars, 1973), 30–1.

23. Cited in Deirdre Bair, *Samuel Beckett: A Biography* (London: Jonathan Cape, 1978), 132.

24. Samuel Beckett, *Disjecta: Miscellaneous Writings and a Dramatic Fragment*, ed. Ruby Cohn (London: John Calder, 1983), 171–2.

25. *Disjecta*, 149.

26. See Bair, *passim*.

Chapter 2

1. I am using 'Ascendancy' here in the conventional sense: that is, to refer to the Anglo-Irish Protestant landed class, a social and political élite which, from the eighteenth century, possessed immense local power in Ireland. The term 'Protestant ascendancy' was first used in the 1780s. The ambiguities of its various usages are analysed by W. J. McCormack in *Ascendancy and Tradition in Anglo-Irish*

Literary History from 1789 to 1939 (Oxford: Clarendon Press, 1985).

2. Seamus Deane, *Celtic Revivals* (London: Faber and Faber, 1985), 28–37.

3. Ibid. 31.

4. A similar point is made by C. L. Innes in her chapter on Elizabeth Bowen in *Woman and Nation in Irish Literature and Society 1880–1935* (London: Harvester Wheatsheaf, 1993), 165–77, where she registers differences of attitude and conception in specifically gendered terms.

5. See Terence Brown, *Ireland: A Social and Cultural History 1922–1985* (London: Fontana, 1985), 110.

6. Polly Devlin, 'Introduction' to *Two Days in Aragon* (London: Virago Press, 1985), p. vii.

7. David Thomson, *Woodbrook* (London: Vintage, 1991; first published in 1974), 26.

8. Elizabeth Bowen, *The Mulberry Tree*, ed. Hermione Lee (London: Virago, 1986), 26.

9. Ibid.

10. Elizabeth Bowen, *The Last September* (Harmondsworth: Penguin, 1982; first published 1929), 119.

11. Elizabeth Bowen, 'Ireland Agonistes', *Europa*, 1 (1971), 59.

12. Cited in Ronald Binns, *J. G. Farrell* (London: Methuen, 1986), 34.

Chapter 3

1. E. M. Forster, 'Introductory Note', in Maurice O'Sullivan, *Twenty Years A-Growing* (Oxford: Oxford University Press, 1953), p. v.

2. See Terence Brown, *Ireland: A Social and Cultural History, 1922–1985* (London: Fontana Press, 1985), ch. 2.

3. Cited ibid. 146.

4. Patrick Kavanagh, *Tarry Flynn* (Harmondsworth: Penguin, 1978; first published 1948), 139.

5. A very well-received dramatic adaptation of the poem by Tom MacIntyre was first performed in 1983. See Patrick Kavanagh and Tom MacIntyre, *The Great Hunger: Poem into Play* (Dublin: The Lilliput Press, 1988).

6. See, for instance, Antoinette Quinn's excellent *Patrick Kavanagh: Born-Again Romantic* (Dublin: Gill and Macmillan, 1991), ch. 4.

7. See Brown, *Ireland,* ch. 2.

8. *Kavanagh's Weekly,* 24 May 1952.

9. See Fredric Jameson, *The Political Unconscious: Narrative as a Socially Symbolic Act* (London: Methuen, 1981).

10. Seamus Heaney, *Preoccupations* (London: Faber and Faber, 1980), 37.

11. Seamus Heaney, *The Government of the Tongue* (London: Faber and Faber, 1988), 7.

12. See Seamus Heaney, 'Place and Displacement: Reflections on Some Recent Poetry from Northern Ireland', in Elmer Andrews (ed.), *Contemporary Irish Poetry: A Collection of Critical Essays* (London: Macmillan, 1992), 124–44.

13. Frank O'Connor, *The Lonely Voice: A Study of the Short Story* (London: Macmillan, 1965), 18, 19.

14. Sean O'Faolain, *Vive Moi!*, rev. edn. (London: Sinclair-Stevenson, 1993; first published 1963), 258.

15. *The Lonely Voice,* 19.

16. It is notable, however, that in her book of reminiscences *Presentation Parlour* (1963) the school run by the Presentation sisters, two of whom were her aunts, is distinctly non-select.

17. Edna O'Brien, *Girls in their Married Bliss* (first published 1964), in *The Country Girls Trilogy* (Harmondsworth: Penguin, 1988), 473.

18. *The Dark* was actually written, but not published, before *The Barracks*.

19. In his excellent introduction to the plays Fintan O'Toole notes the similarity of the situation of *Conversations* to that of Sartre's existentialist play *Huis Clos*, 'in which a room becomes the God-forsaken Hell of other people'. See the introduction to Tom Murphy, *Plays Two* (London: Methuen, 1993).

20. Ibid.

21. Colm Toibin, *The Heather Blazing* (London: Picador, 1992), 32.

Chapter 4

1. Kinsella is quoting the phrase 'asinine feast of sowthistles and brambles' from Milton's *Of Education* (1644), which makes the castigation seem more pedagogically satirical.

2. Frank Budgen, *James Joyce and the Making of 'Ulysses'* (Oxford University Press, 1972; first published in 1934), 69.

3. The contemporaneity of *Ulysses* is informatively discussed by James Fairhall in *James Joyce and the Question of History* (Cambridge: Cambridge University Press, 1993).

4. Fintan O'Toole writes with great perspicacity when he says of these tenements that they are 'a rural setting in urban guise'; and his whole argument in 'Going West: The Country versus the City in Irish Writing' is apposite. See *The Crane Bag*, 9: 2 (1985), 111–17. Part of the article is reprinted in *The Field Day Anthology*, iii. 654–8.

5. Seamus Deane, *Celtic Revivals* (London: Faber and Faber, 1985), 120.

6. Robert Welch, however, describes Stuart's narrative procedures as 'interrogatory intuitions . . . a *jouissance* of energetic unfolding'. See his *Changing States: Transformations in Modern Irish Writing* (London and New York: Routledge, 1993), 158.

7. Austin Clarke, *Selected Poems*, ed. Hugh Maxton (Dublin: The Lilliput Press, 1991), 10.

8. Although most of the poem was composed late in Clarke's life, some stanzas did appear in *Night and Morning* (1938).

9. Clarke, *Selected Poems*, 251.

10. James Joyce, *Ulysses* (Harmondsworth: Penguin Books, 1992; first published in 1922), 42.

11. Eavan Boland, 'Downstream', *Tracks*, 7 [Thomas Kinsella issue] (1987), 23.

12. Eavan Boland, *Object Lessons: The Life of the Woman and the Poet in Our Time* (Manchester: Carcanet Press, 1995), 99, 100.

13. Ibid. 217.

14. But see Edna Longley's subtle argument, in *The Living Stream: Poetry and Revisionism* (Newcastle upon Tyne: Bloodaxe Books, 1994), 187–8, that Boland's work in fact re-inscribes the nationalist ideology which it apparently flouts.

15. Patrick Crotty (ed.), *Modern Irish Poetry: An Anthology* (Belfast: The Blackstaff Press, 1995), 286.

16. Ferdia MacAnna, 'The Dublin Renaissance', *The Irish Review*, 10 (Spring 1991), 14–30.

17. Ibid. 18.

18. Ibid. 29.

19. Dermot Bolger, *The Journey Home* (Harmondsworth: Penguin, 1991; first published 1990), 291.

20. Roddy Doyle, *The Van* (London: Minerva, 1992; first published 1991), 182.

Chapter 5

1. Stewart Parker, 'Introduction' to Sam Thompson, *Over the Bridge* (Dublin: Gill and Macmillan, 1970), 10.

2. See Derek Mahon (ed.), *The Sphere Book of Modern Irish Poetry* (London: Sphere, 1972), 14.

3. Michael Longley, 'Introduction' to Louis MacNeice, *Selected Poems* (London: Faber and Faber, 1988), p. xviii.

4. There are, however, some major exceptions to this in Hewitt's *œuvre*, one being the poem 'A Country Walk in May', published in 1960, which is bluntly sectarian in its definition of the characteristics of the 'black-browed, moody Gaels'. See John Hewitt, *Collected Poems*, ed. Frank Ormsby (Belfast: The Blackstaff Press, 1991), 518.

5. Brian Moore, *Lies of Silence* (London: Vintage, 1992; first published 1990), 70.

6. Terence Brown, *Ireland's Literature* (Mullingar: The Lilliput Press, 1988), 178.

7. Seamus Heaney, 'The Interesting Case of Nero, Chekhov's Cognac and a Knocker', in *The Government of the Tongue* (London: Faber and Faber, 1988), p. xxi.

8. Derek Mahon, 'Poetry in Northern Ireland', *Twentieth Century Studies*, 4 (1970), 92.

9. Seamus Heaney, *Preoccupations: Selected Prose 1968–1978* (London: Faber and Faber, 1980), 56.

10. Bernard O'Donoghue, 'Involved Imaginings: Tom Paulin', in Neil Corcoran (ed.), *The Chosen Ground: Essays on the Contemporary Poetry of Northern Ireland* (Bridgend: Seren Books, 1992), 179.

11. Benedict Kiely, *Nothing Happens in Carmincross* (London: Methuen, 1986; first published 1985), 39.

12. Glenn Patterson, *Fat Lad* (London: Minerva, 1993; first published 1992), 249.

13. Seamus Deane, Introduction to *Selected Plays of Brian Friel* (London: Faber and Faber, 1984), 22. *Translations* is discussed in Chapter 1, above.

14. Frank McGuinness, *'Carthaginians' and 'Baglady'* (London: Faber and Faber, 1988), 69.

Further Reading

1. Political and Cultural History

BARDON, JONATHAN, *A History of Ulster* (Belfast: The Blackstaff Press, 1992).

BARTLETT, THOMAS *et al.* (ed.), *Irish Studies: A General Introduction* (Dublin: Gill and Macmillan, 1988).

BROWN, TERENCE, *Ireland: A Social and Cultural History 1922–1985* (London: Fontana, 1985).

FOSTER, R. F., *Modern Ireland 1600–1972* (London: Allen Lane, The Penguin Press, 1988).

——(ed.), *The Oxford Illustrated History of Ireland* (Oxford: Oxford University Press, 1989).

LEE, J. J., *Ireland 1912–1985: Politics and Society* (Cambridge: Cambridge University Press, 1989).

LYONS, F. S. L., *Ireland Since the Famine* (London: Weidenfeld and Nicolson, 1971; revised edn. Fontana, 1973).

——*Culture and Anarchy in Ireland 1890–1939* (Oxford: Oxford University Press, 1982).

WICHERT, SABINE, *Northern Ireland Since 1945* (London: Longman, 1991).

2. Literary Criticism

Note: There are, of course, numerous books on the individual writers and texts covered in this study. I itemize here only the more general studies of the literature of the period. Many of these include extensive bibliographies of their own.

ALLEN, MICHAEL and ANGELA WILCOX (eds.), *Critical Approaches to Anglo-Irish Literature* (Gerrards Cross: Colin Smythe, 1989).

ANDREWS, ELMER (ed.), *Contemporary Irish Poetry: A Collection of Critical Essays* (London: Macmillan, 1990).

BROWN, TERENCE, *Ireland's Literature: Selected Essays* (Mullingar: The Lilliput Press, 1988).

——and NICHOLAS GRENE (eds.), *Tradition and Influence in Anglo-Irish Poetry* (London: Macmillan, 1989).

CAHALAN, JAMES M., *The Irish Novel: A Critical History* (Dublin: Gill and Macmillan, 1988).

CAIRNS, DAVID and SHAUN RICHARDS, *Writing Ireland: Colonialism, Nationalism and Culture* (Manchester: Manchester University Press, 1988).

CARLSON, JULIA, *Banned in Ireland: Censorship and the Irish Writer* (London: Routledge, 1990).

CONNOLLY, PETER (ed.), *Literature and the Changing Ireland* (Gerrards Cross: Colin Smythe, 1982).

CORCORAN, NEIL, *The Chosen Ground: Essays on the Contemporary Poetry of Northern Ireland* (Bridgend: Seren, 1992).

——*English Poetry since 1940* (Harlow: Longman, 1993).

COUGHLAN, PATRICIA and ALEX DAVIS (eds.), *Modernism and Ireland: The Poetry of the 1930s* (Cork: University of Cork Press, 1995).

CRONIN, JOHN, *Irish Fiction 1900–1940* (Belfast: Appletree Press, 1992).

CRONIN, MICHAEL, *Translating Ireland: Translation, Languages, Cultures* (Cork: Cork University Press, 1996).

DAWE, GERALD, *Against Piety: Essays in Irish Poetry* (Belfast: Lagan Press, 1995).

——and JOHN WILSON FOSTER, *The Poet's Place: Ulster Literature and Society* (Belfast: Institute of Irish Studies, 1991).

DEANE, SEAMUS, *Celtic Revivals: Essays in Modern Irish Literature 1880–1980* (London: Faber and Faber, 1985).

——*A Short History of Irish Literature* (London: Hutchinson, 1986).

——(ed.), *The Field Day Anthology of Irish Writing* (Derry: Field Day Publications, 1991).

DONOGHUE, DENIS, *We Irish: Essays on Irish Literature and Society* (Berkeley: University of California Press, 1986).

DUNN, DOUGLAS (ed.), *Two Decades of Irish Writing* (Manchester: Carcanet Press, 1975).

EAGLETON, TERRY, *Heathcliff and the Great Hunger: Studies in Irish Culture* (London: Verso, 1995).

ETHERTON, MICHAEL, *Contemporary Irish Dramatists* (London: Macmillan, 1989).

FOSTER, JOHN WILSON, *Colonial Consequences: Essays in Irish Literature and Culture* (Dublin: The Lilliput Press, 1991).

GARRATT, ROBERT F., *Modern Irish Poetry: Tradition and Continuity from Yeats to Heaney* (Berkeley: University of California Press, 1986).

GRIFFITHS, TREVOR R. and MARGARET LLEWELYN-JONES (eds.), *British and Irish Women Playwrights since 1958* (Milton Keynes: Open University Press, 1993).

HABERSTROH, PATRICIA BOYLE, *Women Creating Women: Contemporary Irish Women Poets* (Dublin: Attic Press, 1996).

HEALY, ELIZABETH, *Literary Tour of Ireland* (Dublin: Wolfhound Press, 1995).

HEANEY, SEAMUS, *Preoccupations: Selected Prose 1968–1978* (London: Faber and Faber, 1980).

——*The Place of Writing* (Atlanta: Scolars Press, 1989).

HILDEBIDLE, JOHN, *Five Irish Writers: The Errand of Keeping Alive* (Cambridge, Mass.: Harvard University Press, 1989).

HYLAND, PAUL and NEIL SAMMELLS, *Irish Writing: Exile and Subversion* (London: Macmillan, 1991).

INNES, C. L., *Woman and Nation in Irish Literature and Society 1880–1935* (London: Harvester Wheatsheaf, 1993).

JEFFARES, A. NORMAN, *Anglo-Irish Literature* (London: Macmillan, 1982).

JOHNSON, TONI O'BRIEN and DAVID CAIRNS, *Gender in Irish Writing* (Milton Keynes: Open University Press, 1991).

JOHNSTON, DILLON, *Irish Poetry after Joyce* (Notre Dame: University of Notre Dame Press, 1985).

KEARNEY, RICHARD, *Transitions: Narratives in Modern Irish Culture* (Manchester: Manchester University Press, 1988).

KENNEALLY, MICHAEL, *Poetry in Contemporary Irish Literature* (Gerrard Cross: Colin Smythe, 1995).

——(ed.), *Cultural Contexts and Literary Idioms in Contemporary Irish Literature* (Gerrards Cross: Colin Smythe, 1988).

KIBERD, DECLAN, *Inventing Ireland: The Literature of the Modern Nation* (London: Jonathan Cape, 1995).

KINSELLA, THOMAS, *The Dual Tradition: An Essay on Poetry and Politics in Ireland* (Manchester: Carcanet, 1995).

KIRKLAND, RICHARD, *Literature and Culture in Northern Ireland Since 1965: Moments of Danger* (London: Longman, 1996).

LLOYD, DAVID, *Anomalous States: Irish Writing and the Post-Colonial Moment* (Dublin: The Lilliput Press, 1993).

LONGLEY, EDNA, *Poetry in the Wars* (Newcastle: Bloodaxe Books, 1986).

——*The Living Stream: Literature and Revisionism in Ireland* (Newcastle: Bloodaxe Books, 1994).

McCORMACK, W. J., *Ascendancy and Tradition in Anglo-Irish Literary History from 1789 to 1939* (Oxford: Clarendon Press, 1985).

MATTHEWS, STEVEN, *Irish Poetry: Politics, History, Negotiation* (London: Macmillan, 1997).

MAXWELL, D. E. S., *A Critical History of Modern Irish Drama 1891–1980* (Cambridge: Cambridge University Press, 1984).

MERCIER, VIVIAN, *Modern Irish Literature: Sources and Founders* (Oxford: Clarendon Press, 1994).

PAULIN, TOM, *Ireland and the English Crisis* (Newcastle: Bloodaxe Books, 1984).

——*Writing to the Moment: Selected Critical Essays 1980–1996* (London: Faber and Faber, 1996).

RICHTARIK, MARILYNN J., *Acting Between the Lines: The Field Day Theatre Company and Irish Cultural Politics 1980–1984* (Oxford: Clarendon Press, 1994).

ROCHE, ANTHONY, *Contemporary Irish Drama: From Beckett to McGuinness* (Dublin: Gill and Macmillan, 1994).

SEKINE, MASARU (ed.), *Irish Writers and Society at Large* (Gerrards Cross: Colin Smythe, 1985).

STOREY, MARK, *Poetry and Ireland since 1800: A Source Book* (London: Routledge, 1988).

TODD, LORETO, *The Language of Irish Literature* (London: Macmillan, 1989).

TREVOR, WILLIAM, *A Writer's Ireland: Landscape in Literature* (London: Thames and Hudson, 1984).

VANCE, NORMAN, *Irish Literature: A Social History* (Oxford: Basil Blackwell, 1990).

WATSON, G. J., *Irish Identity and the Literary Revival: Synge, Yeats, Joyce and O'Casey* (1979; 2nd edn. Washington, DC: The Catholic University of America Press, 1994).

WELCH, ROBERT, *Changing States: Transformations in Modern Irish Writing* (London: Routledge, 1993).

——(ed.), *The Oxford Companion to Irish Literature* (Oxford: Clarendon Press, 1996).

WILLS, CLAIR, *Improprieties: Politics and Sexuality in Northern Irish Poetry* (Oxford: Clarendon Press, 1993).

WORTH, KATHARINE, *The Irish Drama of Europe from Yeats to Beckett* (London: The Athlone Press, 1978).

Index

820.9　　　Corcoran, Neil.
Cor

　　　　　After Yeats and
　　　　　Joyce.